impact

4

SERIES EDITORS
JoAnn (Jodi) Crandall
Joan Kang Shin

AUTHOR
Thomas Fast

NATIONAL GEOGRAPHIC LEARNING | CENGAGE Learning·

Australia • Brazil • Mexico • Singapore • United Kingdom • United States

Thank you to the educators who provided invaluable feedback during the development of *Impact*:

EXPERT PANEL

Márcia Ferreira, Academic Coordinator, CCBEU, Franca, Brazil

Jianwei Song, Vice-general Manager, Ensure International Education, Harbin, China

María Eugenia Flores, Academic Director, and **Liana Rojas-Binda**, Head of Recruitment & Training, Centro Cultural Costarricense-Norteamericano, San José, Costa Rica

Liani Setiawati, M.Pd., SMPK 1 BPK PENABUR Bandung, Bandung, Indonesia

Micaela Fernandes, Head of Research and Development Committee and Assessment Committee, Pui Ching Middle School, Macau

Héctor Sánchez Lozano, Academic Director, and **Carolina Tripodi**, Head of the Juniors Program, Proulex, Guadalajara, Mexico

Rosario Giraldez, Academic Director, Alianza Cultural, Montevideo, Uruguay

REVIEWERS

BRAZIL

Renata Cardoso, Colégio do Sol, Guara, DF

Fábio Delano Vidal Carneiro, Colégio Sete de Setembro, Fortaleza

Cristiano Carvalho, Centro Educacional Leonardo da Vinci, Vitória

Silvia Corrêa, Associação Alumni, São Paulo

Carol Espinosa, Associação Cultural Brasil Estados Unidos, Salvador

Marcia Ferreira, Centro Cultural Brasil Estados Unidos, Franca

Clara Haddad, ELT Consultant, São Paulo

Elaine Carvalho Chaves Hodgson, Colégio Militar de Brasília, Brasília

Thays Farias Galvão Ladosky, Associação Brasil América, Recife

Itana Lins, Colégio Anchieta, Salvador

Samantha Mascarenhas, Associação Cultural Brasil Estados Unidos, Salvador

Ann Marie Moreira, Pan American School of Bahia, Bahia

Rodrigo Ramirez, CEETEPS- Fatec Zona Sul, São Paulo

Paulo Torres, Vitória Municipality, Vitória

Renata Zainotte, Go Up Idiomas, Rio de Janeiro

CHINA

Zhou Chao, MaxEn Education, Beijing

Zhu Haojun, Only International Education, Shanghai

Su Jing, Beijing Chengxun International English School, Beijing

Jianjun Shen, Phoenix City International School, Guangzhou

COSTA RICA

Luis Antonio Quesada-Umaña, Centro Cultural Costarricense Norteamericano, San José

INDONESIA

Luz S. Ismail, M.A., LIA Institute of Language and Vocational Training, Jakarta

Selestin Zainuddin, LIA Institute of Language and Vocational Training, Jakarta

Rosalia Dian Devitasari, SMP Kolese Kanisius, Jakarta

JAPAN

John Williams, Tezukayama Gakuen, Nara

MEXICO

Nefertiti González, Instituto Mexicano Madero, Puebla

Eugenia Islas, Instituto Tlalpan, Mexico City

Marta MM Seguí, Colegio Velmont A.C., Puebla

SOUTH KOREA

Min Yuol (Alvin) Cho, Global Leader English Education, Yong In

THAILAND

Panitnan Kalayanapong, Eduzone Co., Ltd., Bangkok

TURKEY

Damla Çaltuğ, İELEV, Istanbul

Basak Nalcakar Demiralp, Ankara Sinav College, Ankara

Humeyra Olcayli, İstanbul Bilim College, Istanbul

VIETNAM

Chantal Kruger, ILA Vietnam, Hô Chí Minh

Ai Nguyen Huynh, Vietnam USA Society, Hô Chí Minh

impact

4

	1 Pushing the Limits	**2 It Takes a Village**	**3 Food Matters**	**4 The Footprint of Fun**
THEME	Pushing mental and physical limits	Digital humanitarianism and crowdsourcing	Food sustainability	The environmental impact of entertainment
VOCABULARY STRATEGIES	· Prefix *un-* · Use a dictionary	· Suffixes *-ion, -tion* · Identify parts of speech	· Borrowed words · Use context of unit	· Prefix *pro-* · Use context of sentence
SPEAKING STRATEGY	Showing interest in a conversation	Making suggestions and agreeing or disagreeing	Offering advice and accepting or declining advice	Defending your opinion
GRAMMAR	**Embedded clauses, questions, and commands** *I think extreme sports are dangerous.* **Adding emphasis** *The reason (why) I won't go surfing is that I don't like swimming in the ocean.*	**Future tenses:** Describing events in the future *Over the next few years, people will look online to find volunteers to help with disaster relief.* **Quantifiers:** Expressing amounts *Half of/Fifty percent of the world's population is . . .*	**Mixed conditionals:** Expressing how things would be different *If I hadn't learned about overfishing, I would still be eating tuna.* **Double comparatives:** Describing outcomes *The more people there are in the world, the more food we need to produce.*	**Passives:** Describing actions and processes *What has been done by musicians to reduce their ecological footprint?* **Verbs followed by gerunds or infinitives** *Parks must continue coming up with/to come up with ways to reuse water.*
READING	*No Limits*	*Focus on the Future*	*Grow It Here, Eat It Here*	*Game Over*
READING STRATEGY	Summarize	Use text features for comprehension	Connect text to prior knowledge	Identify author's purpose
VIDEO	*A Tribute to Discomfort*	*Crisis Mapping*	*Should We Eat More Bugs?*	*The Footprint of Fans*
WRITING	Genre: **Biography** Focus: Identify chronological order	Genre: **Persuasive essay** Focus: Express point of view	Genre: **Restaurant review** Focus: Use facts and opinions to review	Genre: **Problem and solution essay** Focus: Present facts and personal reflection
MISSION	**Test Your Limits** National Geographic Photography Fellow: **Cory Richards**, Photojournalist	**Do Your Part** National Geographic Explorer: **Patrick Meier**, Crisis Mapper	**Know Your Food** National Geographic Explorer: **Barton Seaver**, Chef/Conservationist	**Reduce Your Footprint** National Geographic Ambassador to the Arts: **Jack Johnson**, Musician
PRONUNCIATION	Intonation in embedded *yes/no* questions	Stress in compound nouns	The letter *t* between vowels	Expressing emotions with intonation
EXPRESS YOURSELF	Creative Expression: **Graphic novel** *The Adventures of Crisis Crusher* Making connections: Pushing limits while working to help others		Creative Expression: **Online invitation** *Reduce, Reuse, Recycle, Rock!* Making connections: Sustainable eating and fun	

Unit 1

CORY RICHARDS **Photojournalist**

Cory Richards takes pictures all over the world. He uses these photos to tell stories about people and places around the world. He's been to all seven continents, climbed some of the tallest mountains on Earth, and hiked in below-freezing temperatures. Cory has overcome extreme obstacles and has pushed himself to his limit. He doesn't mind being out of his comfort zone. Do you?

Unit 2

PATRICK MEIER **Crisis Mapper**

Did you know that social media posts, text messages, and emails can save lives? Thanks to crisis mappers like Patrick Meier, people affected by natural disasters can get help faster. Patrick sorts through their communication and creates crisis maps that he shares with rescue teams. Patrick believes that, when people collaborate and use technology, they can make a difference.

Unit 3

BARTON SEAVER **Chef/Conservationist**

Barton Seaver wants you to think about what you eat. As a chef and conservationist, Barton has traveled all over the world to cook and eat different foods. He likes to learn about people and cultures through food. Now he works to raise awareness about healthy eating and seafood sustainability.

Unit 4

JACK JOHNSON **Musician**

Jack Johnson is a musician, surfer, and environmentalist. He uses his music to promote sustainability and conservation. Jack travels to his concerts in biofuel buses and promotes sustainable local food at his shows. Jack proves that being green and having fun can go hand-in-hand. What do you like to do for "green fun"?

Unit 5

COREY JASKOLSKI **Engineer/Inventor**

Corey Jaskolski is an engineer who creates technologies so that people can virtually explore the world. With his 360-degree camera, anyone can explore inside of King Tut's tomb without harming its artifacts or swim in the deep ocean alongside the sharks without leaving home. Corey's gadgets help explorers protect what they discover. Do you use technology to explore?

Unit 6

NIZAR IBRAHIM **Paleontologist**

Nizar Ibrahim is German/Moroccan and as a kid in Germany, he wanted to learn about dinosaurs. He's lucky because now that's his job as he searches for dinosaurs in Morocco. He decided to hunt for dinosaurs there because very little research has been done in the Sahara Desert. Imagine how excited he was to find fossils of a prehistoric giant, *Spinosaurus*.

Unit 7

TAN LE **Innovator/Entrepreneur**

Have you ever wanted to be able to move objects with your mind? Tan Le created a portable brain scanner that can do just that! It also helps doctors better understand the healthy human brain. Tan went through a long process of trial and error before her brain scanner worked, which taught her that failure is a step toward success.

Unit 8

STEPHEN ALVAREZ **Photographer**

Photographer Stephen Alvarez believes art has the power to connect people across time and distance—even from the prehistoric world to people today. In 2014, he photographed ancient art in the Chauvet-Pont-d'Arc cave in France. These paintings were made 36,000 years ago! Stephen felt very connected to the ancient artists that created them. Does art help you connect with others?

Pushing the Limits

Free-climbing the Dawn Wall in
Yosemite National Park, United States

"We have to learn how
far we can go."
—Cory Richards

1. Look at the climber. Why would he choose to climb
   this rock? What are some of the risks he faces?

2. What is the most challenging sport you've ever tried?

3. Why should we challenge ourselves? What is a
   benefit of taking risks?

1 **Why do we take risks?** Discuss. Then listen and read. TR: 2

Have you ever **pushed yourself** to your **limit**? Do you know anyone who has? Do you ever wonder what can be gained by climbing a tall cliff—or jumping off it? Why do something that causes the body **pain**?

People can be transformed by pushing themselves. These experiences teach **determination**. Often, the desire to achieve our goal **enables** us to take risks. Many people take mild risks. Others feel a need to reach the unreachable. These **extreme** athletes test their own **mental** and **physical** boundaries.

In most traditional sports, athletes compete against one another. But in extreme sports, the biggest **opponent** is nature. In this photo, Olympic snowboarder Jussi Oksanen glides down the side of a glacier. Snowboarding on solid ice is **hazardous**, especially with a 12 m (40 ft.) drop below the glacier! But for extreme athletes like Oksanen, risk is just part of the job.

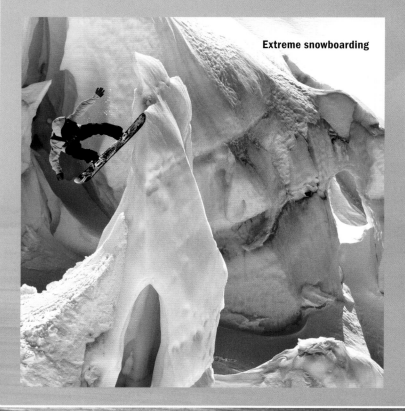

Extreme snowboarding

Big-wave surfing

The same is true for big-wave surfers. Animals such as sharks and jellyfish pose serious risks to surfers. Another **obstacle** that surfers must **overcome** is the force of the water. After this photo was taken, surfer Koa Rothman was taken under by the unbelievable force of the wave. So why do it? "The view I had right here was one of the most amazing things I have ever seen in my life," says Koa. "Being in the middle of all that energy is unexplainable!"

Athletes who participate in the *Marathon des Sables*, or MdS, need to have incredible **endurance**. In this desert marathon, participants must cross a distance of approximately 250 km (155 mi.) over five or six days. The event takes place in the Sahara Desert, where temperatures can reach more than 50°C (122°F). It's no wonder that the MdS is considered the toughest race on Earth!

The athletes shown in the photos are **role models** for anyone seeking adventure. Do they inspire you to push your own limits?

Desert-marathon running

2 **Learn new words.** Listen and repeat. TR: 3

3 **Work in pairs.** Which of these sports would you try? Why would you try it? What risks would you face?

4 **Read and write the words from the list.** Make any necessary changes.

determination	hazardous	mental	obstacle	opponent
overcome	pain	physical	push himself	role model

Photographer and adventurer Cory Richards is used to difficult conditions. Cory has _____ many difficult _____ to bring us some incredible outdoor action photography. Cory believes that pushing his _____ and _____ limits helps him to better connect with himself and with the world.

In 2011, Cory successfully climbed an 8,000 m (26,000 ft.) peak in the middle of winter. However, due to the _____ conditions, this challenge nearly cost him his life. On the way down, Cory and his team were caught in a major avalanche. "Once the avalanche took us, there was no more fear," says Cory. Although this experience scared him, he still takes risks to get a great photo. Cory's _____ and endurance make him a great _____ .

5 **Learn new words.** Listen to the words and match them to the definitions. Then listen and repeat. TR: 4 and 5

to achieve	boundary	unbelievable	unreachable

_____ 1. incredible

_____ 2. limit

_____ 3. do

_____ 4. impossible

Cory Richards

6 **Choose an activity. Work in pairs.**

1. Talk about characteristics that adventurers like Cory need to have. Which of these characteristics do you have? Which would you like to have?

2. Role-play an interview between a TV reporter and an extreme athlete who has just completed a new challenge.

3. Invent an extreme sport. Work together to make a poster describing a competition for this sport.

Showing interest in a conversation

Statement	Responses
I love to surf.	Wow! What's that like?
	No way! I never knew that <u>you could surf</u>.
	What can you tell me about <u>surfing</u>?
	Tell me more about <u>how you learned to surf</u>.
	What about you? Do you like <u>extreme sports</u>?
	You're <u>a surfer</u>? Me, too!

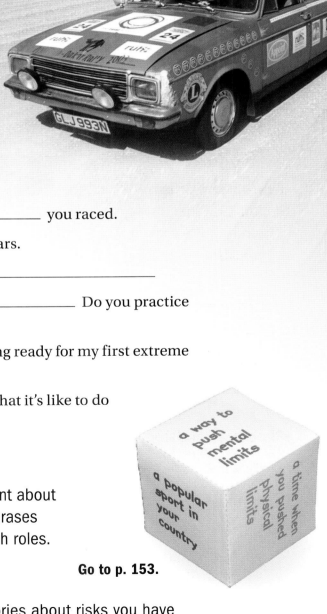

7 **Listen.** How do these speakers show interest in the conversation? Write the phrases you hear. TR: 7

8 **Read and complete the dialogue.**

Lee: What are you doing, Jon?

Jon: I'm getting ready for my next mountain bike race.

Lee: No way! _____ you raced.

Jon: Yeah, I've been racing for about three years.

Lee: _____

Jon: It's very cool. _____ Do you practice extreme sports?

Lee: Yeah, I like rock climbing. And I'm getting ready for my first extreme ironing competition.

Jon: _____ what it's like to do extreme ironing.

Lee: I can't yet—I've never done it!

9 **Work in pairs.** Toss the cube. Make a statement about the topic on the cube. Your partner uses the phrases above to maintain the conversation. Then switch roles.

a way to push mental limits

a popular sport in your country

a time when you pushed physical limits

Go to p. 153.

10 **Work in groups.** Do you take risks? Share stories about risks you have taken. Tell one true story and one false story. See if your group can guess the true story. Use the phrases above to maintain the conversations.

Embedded clauses, questions, and commands

I think . . . Extreme sports are dangerous.	**I think extreme sports are** dangerous.
I wonder . . . What obstacles has Cory overcome?	**I wonder what obstacles Cory has overcome.**
Do you know . . . Can we climb that mountain in winter?	**Do you know if we can climb** that mountain in winter?
I'm asking you . . . Try downhill mountain biking.	**I'm asking you to try** downhill mountain biking.

11 **Work independently.** Listen to the speakers. Then complete the embedded clause, question, or command. Remember to change the order of words when necessary. **TR: 9**

1. She's guessing _____

2. He's wondering _____

3. You're telling me _____

4. I think _____

5. I'm asking you _____

12 **Work in pairs.** Make sentences to form embedded clauses, questions, and commands.

I wonder	Wear a helmet when you ride your bike.
I think	Had Cory been in an avalanche before?
I'm asking	Teach your brother how to surf.
I'm telling	How many countries has Cory visited?
Do you remember if	You could try ice climbing.

1. _____

2. _____

3. _____

4. _____

5. _____

13 **Learn new words.** You've learned about physical challenges. Now listen and read about a mental challenge. Then listen and repeat. TR: 10 and 11

A **nontraditional** sport, such as ice climbing, can really push us to our physical limits. But, have you ever done anything that pushes you to your mental limits? Around the world, students participate in tough academic competitions, such as Math Olympiads. These **events** require a lot of training, just as an extreme sport does. The competitions often require students to **struggle** with complex problems. Sometimes it takes over an hour to complete just one!

Nur Muhammad Shafiullah knows first-hand how the Math Olympiads can push mental limits. He is the youngest student ever to compete in the International Mathematical Olympiad. At 15, Nur Muhammad went to the international competition to **represent** his native country, Bangladesh. He competed against students from 125 countries and took the bronze medal! The next year he did it again. The year after that he earned a silver medal. Nur Muhammad's math skills are really unbelievable. What about you? Do you think the International Mathematical Olympiad is beyond your mental limits?

14 **Work in pairs.** Write sentences using the words below. Include an embedded clause, question, or command in each sentence.

1. wonder / time / event   *I wonder if the event takes much time.* _____

2. guessing / struggle / difficult _____

3. think / student / prepare _____

4. telling / nontraditional / sport _____

5. asking / represent / country _____

15 **Work in groups.** Think of other competitions that provide mental challenges. What do you know about them? What questions do you have? Discuss in your group, using embedded clauses, questions, and commands as much as possible.

16 **Before you read, discuss in pairs.** Look at the photos, caption, and title. What do you think this reading is about?

17 **Learn new words.** Find the words below in the reading. What do you think they mean? Use a dictionary to check. Then listen and repeat. TR: 12

> beyond   consequence   in control   limb   peak performance

18 **While you read, pause after each paragraph to write what it's about in your own words.** TR: 13

19 **After you read, work in small groups to answer the questions.**

1. How did Amy lose her legs?
2. What other negative consequences did Amy suffer from meningitis?
3. What happened the first time Amy tried to go snowboarding again?
4. What did Amy learn about limitations?
5. How does Amy work to help others?
6. If she could, would she go back to her former life? Why or why not?

Amy Purdy snowboarding

No Limits

AMY PURDY SEES HER LIMITATIONS AS A GIFT THAT HAS HELPED HER DO AMAZING THINGS.

Amy Purdy is a world-class athlete, model, and actress. She has achieved amazing success in her life and hasn't let anything slow her down—even the loss of both legs! In fact, some of Amy's greatest achievements came after she lost them.

When Amy was 15, she started snowboarding. After finishing high school, she moved to the mountains, where she could easily spend her free time snowboarding. She felt totally in control of her life. But then at 19, she contracted meningitis, a horrible disease that left her with only a two-percent chance of survival. Amy survived, but there were terrible consequences. She lost a kidney, the hearing in her left ear, and both legs below the knees.

For a long time Amy felt depressed. But when she closed her eyes, she could still see herself snowboarding. She decided not to let this situation take over her life. By the time she was 21, she was back on her board, wearing artificial legs she had built herself. The first time she tried to use them, she fell off, but her legs kept going down the hill without her! After a few years of hard training using her new legs, Amy was able to reach her peak performance level. She became the Para-Snowboard World Champion in 2012, and she later won the bronze medal in the 2014 Paralympic Games.

Amy's new life was beyond what she expected. Suddenly, she had become a celebrity, a fashion model, and an actress. She was even on the hit TV show *Dancing with the Stars*. Most importantly, she started helping people like her do the sports they love. She started a company that makes artificial limbs and she created an organization that introduces people with physical disabilities to action sports.

Now, if you ask Amy, "Would you want to change your situation?", she would say no. Losing her legs has enabled, not disabled, her. According to Amy, "It's facing our fears head on that allows us to live our lives beyond our borders."

20 Work in pairs. Reread the text. Then without looking, take turns saying what you remember. Use your own words.

21 Discuss in groups.

1. How did getting meningitis impact Amy's life? Identify positive and negative impacts.
2. Do you agree that disadvantages can become advantages? Explain.
3. Do you think anyone can overcome an obstacle like Amy has? Why or why not? Give examples.

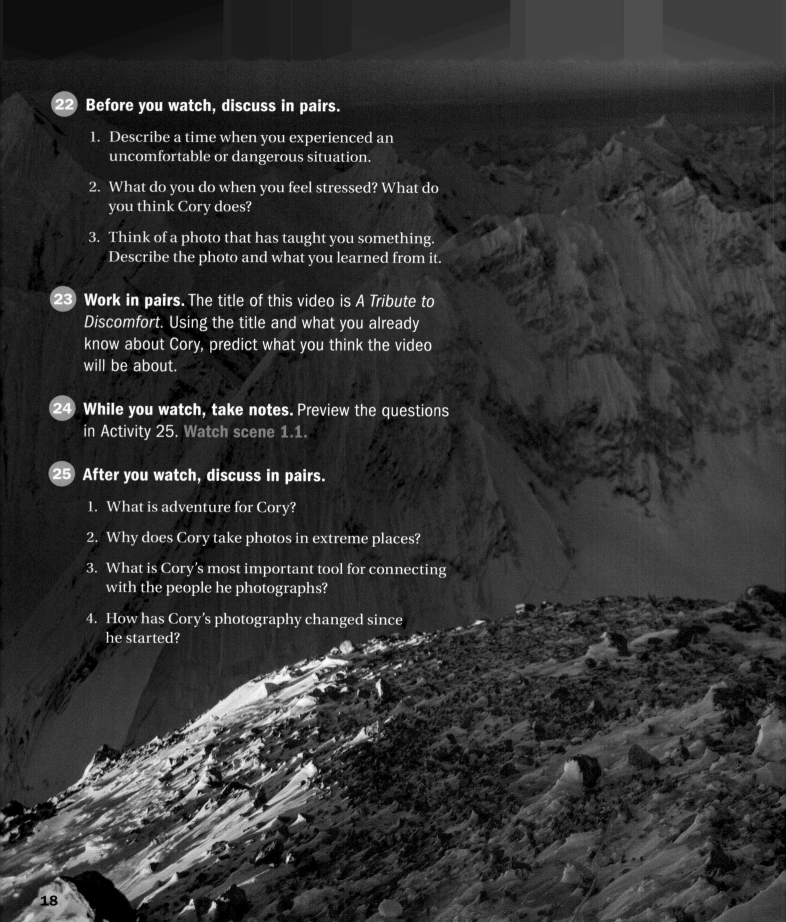

22 **Before you watch, discuss in pairs.**

1. Describe a time when you experienced an uncomfortable or dangerous situation.

2. What do you do when you feel stressed? What do you think Cory does?

3. Think of a photo that has taught you something. Describe the photo and what you learned from it.

23 **Work in pairs.** The title of this video is *A Tribute to Discomfort*. Using the title and what you already know about Cory, predict what you think the video will be about.

24 **While you watch, take notes.** Preview the questions in Activity 25. Watch scene 1.1.

25 **After you watch, discuss in pairs.**

1. What is adventure for Cory?

2. Why does Cory take photos in extreme places?

3. What is Cory's most important tool for connecting with the people he photographs?

4. How has Cory's photography changed since he started?

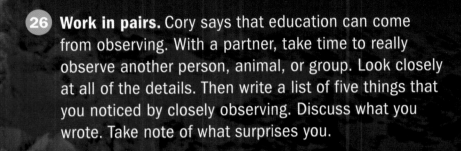

26 **Work in pairs.** Cory says that education can come from observing. With a partner, take time to really observe another person, animal, or group. Look closely at all of the details. Then write a list of five things that you noticed by closely observing. Discuss what you wrote. Take note of what surprises you.

27 **Work in groups.** In the video, Cory mentions the "richness of struggle." Try something that will cause you to struggle or to be uncomfortable. Discuss the positives of this experience.

Cory Richards takes risks to get a good shot. This photo was taken from the top of the 8,034 m (26,360 ft.) Gasherbrum II, in Pakistan.

28 **Choose an activity. Work in pairs.**

1. Research Cory's photography. Share and describe your favorites of his photos with the class.

2. Photography gives Cory a voice. Take a photograph to teach others about someone or something. Share your photo with a partner. Discuss your partner's reactions.

3. Compare and contrast Amy Purdy and Cory Richards. How does each person push him/herself? What obstacles has each person overcome?

19

Adding emphasis

My sister loves to hike in the Himalayas.
The place (where) my sister loves hiking **is** the Himalayas.

I won't go surfing. I don't like swimming in the ocean.
The reason (why) I won't go surfing **is that** I don't like swimming in the ocean.

He loves yoga because it makes him feel relaxed.
The thing (that) he loves about yoga **is that** it makes him feel relaxed.

I like snow kiting. It pushes me to my physical limits.
What I like best about snow kiting **is that** it pushes me to my physical limits.

---

29 **Read.** Then rewrite the sentences to add emphasis.

1. I prefer snowboarding to skiing because I need less equipment.

   The reason why _I prefer snowboarding is that I need less equipment._

2. José really enjoys climbing in the Andes.

   The place _____

3. I love the excitement of kite surfing.

   The thing _____

4. Maria likes trying extreme sports.

   The person _____

5. You should try tae kwon do. It really helps you focus.

   The reason _____

30 **Work in pairs.** Take turns choosing cards from each pile. Discuss the sport pictured on your card. Add emphasis.

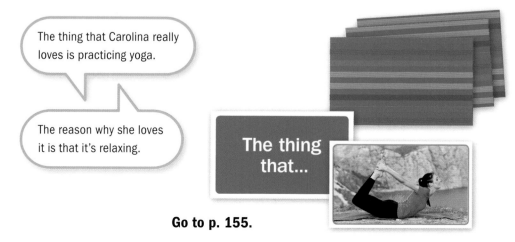

The thing that Carolina really loves is practicing yoga.

The reason why she loves it is that it's relaxing.

The thing that...

Go to p. 155.

WRITING

A biography tells the story of a person's life. Here are some useful words and phrases to connect ideas when writing a biography:

afterwards	**at first**	**eventually**
later on	**more recently**	**ultimately**

31 **Read the model.** Work in pairs to study the writing model. What words does the writer use to organize the biography? Underline them.

Yuko Arimori is an Olympic marathon runner. She was born in Japan in 1966. At first, Arimori had difficulty walking because of a problem with her legs. Other children made fun of her. Her gym teacher helped her to gain confidence, and Arimori learned to try new things, such as running track. Through hard work, she became one of the best high school runners in her city.

Eventually, Arimori tried to join a top track team in Japan. When a spot opened for a marathon runner, Arimori saw her chance. She had never been fast, but speed wasn't as important as endurance, which Arimori had. Ultimately, she became one of the best female marathon runners in the world. In 1992, at the age of 26, she participated in the Barcelona Olympics, where she won the silver medal. Afterwards, in the 1996 Olympics, Arimori won the bronze.

Later on, in 1998, Arimori decided to go beyond just running. She started Hearts of Gold, a volunteer organization to help land mine victims in Cambodia. Hearts of Gold sponsors the Angkor Wat International Half Marathon. Runners from around the world compete to raise money to buy artificial limbs for those who lost arms and legs because of land mines. In fact, many of the victims join the race!

More recently, Arimori was a United Nations Good Will Ambassador. Today, she's the President and CEO of Special Olympics Nippon. She continues to help people in Cambodia and other parts of the world.

32 **Work in pairs.** Identify four phases of Yuko's life.

33 **Write.** Write a biography of an athlete who is a role model for others. Use the words and phrases above to help you organize the biography.

Test Your Limits

"Adventure is anything that puts us outside our comfort zone."
—Cory Richards
National Geographic Photography Fellow, Photojournalist

1. Watch scene 1.2.

2. Cory gets out of his comfort zone by climbing the tallest mountains in the world—in the winter! What takes you out of your comfort zone? Discuss with a partner.

3. How could you get more adventure from your life? What do you think you might learn about yourself by trying something new?

Make an Impact

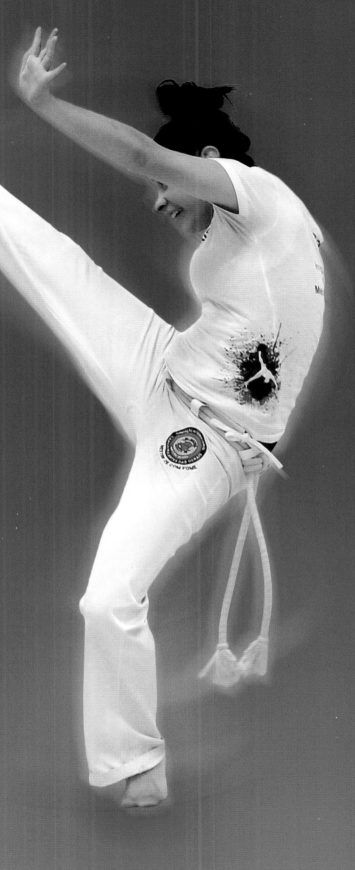

A Try something new!

- Do something you've never done before.

- Write a paragraph to describe your experiences. What did you do? Did it take you outside of your comfort zone? What were the benefits and challenges of this new experience?

- Present a summary of your experience to the class.

B Create an instructional video.

- Choose a particular sport that pushes your limits, such as yoga, martial arts, or distance running.

- Create a video about the sport. Describe how to do the sport. Talk about its mental and physical requirements.

- Film your video and share it with the class.

C Interview a role model.

- Choose a person in your community who is a role model for teens.

- Write at least five questions to use in your interview. Ask about the person's life, what obstacles he/she has overcome, and how he/she has pushed him/herself.

- Conduct your interview. Then, summarize what you learned about the person for your classmates. Share a photo if possible.

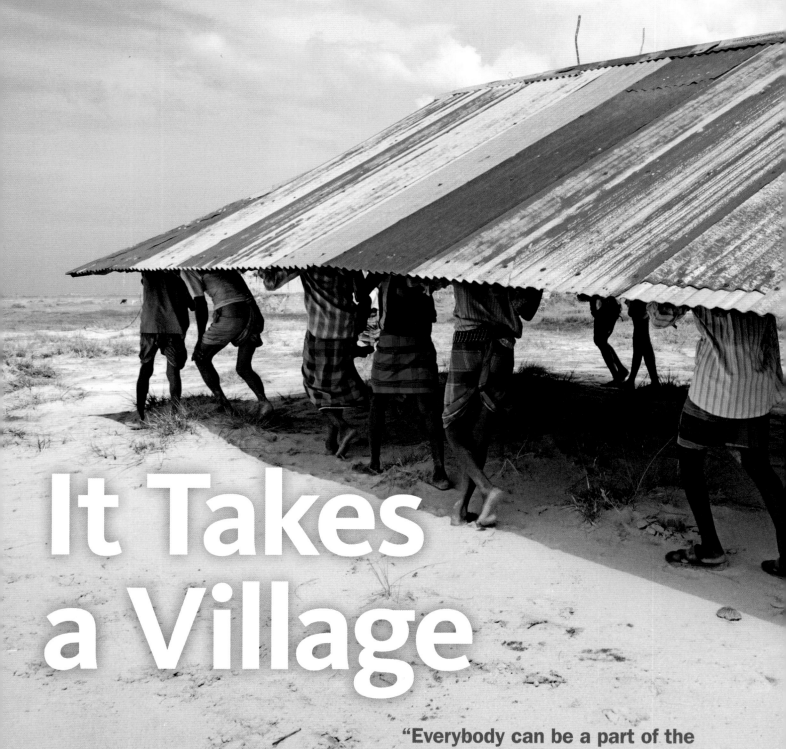

It Takes a Village

"Everybody can be a part of the solution if they want."

—Patrick Meier

Men working together to move a roof, Bangladesh

1. What are the people in the photo doing? Why might they be doing this?

2. Think of a time when you needed someone else's help. Describe the problem. Who helped you? How did they help?

3. People need help after a crisis, such as an earthquake or a powerful storm. What types of things do people need in these situations? How could you help them?

25

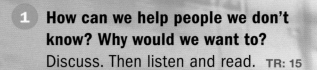

We want to help each other in times of **crisis**. This idea is nothing new. For centuries, our ancestors have worked together to help one another whenever a crisis struck their village. This collaboration brought their communities together. Over time, these communities have **expanded** to become a "global village" of over 7 billion people. When we hear about a massive earthquake or typhoon hitting another part of the world, we still want to help—but how? Crisis mapper Patrick Meier has found a way you can help—without even leaving your home.

Meier has created a network of "digital **humanitarians**" who produce crisis maps that **measure** the **scale** of a disaster and provide the most up-to-date information for what is needed on the ground. They do it through **crowdsourcing**, or transmitting information using online resources and social media.

Patrick Meier analyzes data to help with relief efforts during a storm.

People in the affected area **upload** messages and photos that show **evidence** of disasters immediately after they occur. These updates **generate** an enormous **amount** of **data**, which is sorted by digital humanitarians, and then posted to the crisis map. People working online and on the ground **process** the information and use it to understand **the big picture**. Rescuers use these updates to **monitor** the levels of destruction and coordinate relief for difficult situations. So now when disaster strikes, help can come from anywhere on Earth.

2 **Learn new words.** Listen and repeat. TR: 16

3 **Work in pairs.** Have you ever helped anyone in need? What did you do? Would you use social media to help people you've never met? Why or why not?

27

4 Read and listen. Write the missing words and phrases. TR: 17

Patrick Meier uses _____ maps and social media to organize information and give _____ on what's happening at a disaster site. However, scientists are using other forms of technology to collect _____, to _____ solutions, and to help people in need. Some scientists are developing microbots to explore where humans cannot easily go, such as outer space or inside the human body. Microbots are simple machines, but when released in large _____, they can accomplish a lot. If sent into a disaster area, scientists could _____ their movements and _____ their progress while they search for _____ of life. If one microbot gets lost, the mission could still continue.

A microbot attacking a cancer cell

5 Learn new words. Listen for these words and write them next to the definitions. Then listen and repeat. TR: 18 and 19

collaboration	to coordinate	relief	situation	update

_____ 1. help for victims of a disaster

_____ 2. the process of working together

_____ 3. what is happening at a certain time and place

_____ 4. organize and connect people so they can work together

_____ 5. the latest information

6 Choose an activity.

1. **Work independently.** Write three survey questions about using technology to help crisis victims. Explain the idea of "digital humanitarians" to several friends outside of class, and then have them answer your questions. Present their responses to the class.

2. **Work independently.** Interview a technology expert about how social media technology can be useful in helping people. You could interview a technology teacher at your school, a family member, or another adult you know who works in technology. Present your interview in a magazine article.

3. **Work in groups.** Discuss ways that you can get crowdsourced information from the Internet.

Making suggestions	Agreeing	Disagreeing
I think _____ .	Great idea!	I see what you mean but _____ .
What if we _____ ?	I agree completely.	Wouldn't it be better if _____ ?
Wouldn't it be best to _____ ?	Sure, why not?	But don't you think _____ ?

7 **Listen.** How do the people make and respond to suggestions? Write the phrases you hear. TR: 21

8 **Read and complete the dialogue.**

Alejo: Hey Eva, did you hear about the hurricane in the Caribbean? I've been busy helping out.

Eva: How can you help from far away?

Alejo: I volunteer to read messages and look at photos from the area to decide who needs help.

Eva: _____ I wish there were something I could do.

Alejo: _____ you should help out. _____ work together?

Eva: _____ I would need to be trained? I have no idea what to do!

Alejo: I can show you. It's easy! And you could help a lot of people. What do you think?

Eva: _____

9 **Work in pairs.** Imagine there has been a natural disaster in another country. Student A spins the wheel and makes a suggestion how to help. Student B then spins the wheel to determine whether to agree or disagree. If Student B disagrees, he/she must make a new suggestion.

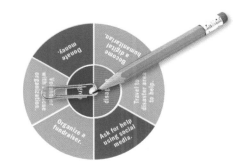

Go to p. 153.

10 **Work in groups.** Talk about organizing a fundraiser in your school to help victims of a natural disaster. Choose a cause and discuss ways to raise money for it. Make and respond to suggestions in your discussion.

Future tenses: Describing events in the future

Over the next few years, people **will look** online to find volunteers to help with disaster relief.

In the upcoming years, researchers **will be working** to develop new technologies that solve global problems.

By 2050, organizations **will have found** new online resources to solve their biggest problems.

11 **Listen.** Write the future-tense forms you hear on the timeline. TR: 23

In 2020, an 8.5 magnitude earthquake

_____

South America.

_____
_____
_____

_____
_____
_____

2020   2030   2040   2050   2060   2070

By 2030, the world population

_____

around 8.3 billion people. World hunger levels

_____

By 2050, many regions in the world

_____

flooded because of rising sea levels.

Toward the end of the century, a massive asteroid

_____

the Earth's orbit.

12 **Work in pairs.** Make two additional predictions for the years 2040 and 2060. Write your answers in the spaces provided on the timeline from Activity 11.

13 **Work in groups.** Look again at predictions on the timeline. Discuss what scientists and everyday people will do to handle these situations. Use the future tenses in your answer.

By 2050, scientists will have found better ways to predict the weather.

And people will be preparing their homes for more hurricanes.

14 **Learn new words.** What can you do to help your neighbors? Read the suggestions for helping in your own community. Then, listen and repeat. TR: 24

What will you do the next time a disaster strikes? You know you can help others without ever leaving your home. But being involved in your community is also important. Over the next year, what will you be doing to help out locally?

Volunteer to clean up a beach or a local park.

Help out at a local library or animal shelter.

Hold a **fundraiser** to raise money for an important **cause**.

Organize and lead a **network** of young volunteers in your community.

15 **Listen.** Write the four activities mentioned in the dialogue. Then, put a ✓ by what the speakers decide to do as community service. TR: 25

_____

_____

_____

_____

16 **Work in pairs.** Brainstorm other ways to help individuals in your community. Include 1–2 examples that would require the use of technology. Which will you be doing? Why?

17 **Work in groups.** Join another pair and compare your ideas from Activity 16. Choose the best overall idea and create a radio or TV commercial to encourage others to volunteer. Use future tenses to explain how the activity will benefit members of your community.

18 **Before you read, discuss in pairs.** Based on the title and the quotation, what do you think the reading is about?

19 **Learn new words.** Find these words in the reading. What do you think they mean? Think about what type of word each one is. Then listen and repeat. **TR: 26**

to empower	to engineer	to face
generation	innovation	

20 **While you read, think about the title, the subtitle, and the quotation.** **TR: 27**

21 **After you read, work in pairs to answer the questions.**

1. What is a problem facing Sierra Leone?
2. What are two of Kelvin's inventions? How do they help others?
3. Why did David bring Kelvin to MIT for three weeks?
4. How does David work to promote innovation among young people?

FOCUS
ON THE
FUTURE

Kelvin Doe, also known as DJ Focus, is creating a future he wants to live in.

Imagine growing up in a place where the electricity is shut off more than it is turned on. Could you do anything to help your community? At eleven years old, Kelvin Doe saw the lack of power in his country, Sierra Leone, as a problem. Kelvin was committed to solving this problem, so he became an inventor.

Kelvin was forced to be creative in his inventions. He could not afford to buy supplies. So he collected broken electronic parts from the trash and taught himself how to engineer new devices. By age thirteen, Kelvin was creating his own batteries by combining acid, soda, and metal in tin cups. His simple invention gave light to a community often left in the dark, and it also led to other innovations.

At fourteen, Kelvin made his own FM radio transmitter and created his community's first local radio station. "If we have a radio station," he said, "the people can debate issues affecting our community and Sierra Leone as a whole." Kelvin, who took the name DJ Focus, quickly developed a group of loyal listeners.

Kelvin's hard work paid off. The national television station in Sierra Leone heard about his inventions and invited him to do a live demonstration on air. Shortly afterward, he was invited to visit the Massachusetts Institute of Technology (MIT) to learn more about creative engineering. That visit was arranged by MIT doctoral student David Sengeh.

Like Kelvin, David grew up in Sierra Leone. He is a researcher at the MIT Media Lab, and founder of the organization Global Minimum, Inc. Through this organization, he aims to empower high school students in Sierra Leone by encouraging innovation. David wants more young Sierra Leoneans to be like Kelvin—to look at the problems their communities face and find ways to solve them so that their generation will have a better future.

Kelvin spent three weeks in the United States, learning from David and other researchers at MIT. At the end of the trip, he was ready to go home and get back to work. "Whatever I've learned here," said Kelvin, "I will share it with my friends, colleagues, and loved ones, and do it as a team."

"How do we create thousands of young people who are inspired by making stuff and solving the problems that are in their neighborhood?"

—David Sengeh, National Geographic Emerging Explorer, Biomedical Engineer

22 **Work in pairs.** Reread the question in the quotation. Discuss why the question is important to David. Then try to answer it.

23 **Discuss in groups.**

1. What is a challenge facing your community? What could be done to solve it? What knowledge do you need to solve it?
2. How do David and Kelvin give back to the people of Sierra Leone? What can they learn from each other?
3. Reread the following: *"Whatever I've learned here, I will share it with my friends, colleagues, and loved ones . . ."* What have you learned that you can share with others? What can you accomplish when you share knowledge?

24 **Before you watch, work in pairs.** Summarize what you've learned so far about crisis mapping. Who is involved? When is it needed? Who does it help?

25 **Read and circle.** The video you're going to watch is called *Crisis Mapping*. Think about what you've learned in this unit, and what you discussed in Activity 24. Then circle the words or phrases from the box that you think you'll hear in the video.

analyze data	digital	explore
police officers	silence	social media
helicopter	update	

26 **Watch scene 2.1. While you watch, outline the steps involved in crisis mapping.**

27 **After you watch, work in pairs.** Put the steps for crisis mapping in order.

_____ Digital humanitarians analyze data from the photos and text messages they receive.

_____ Thanks to the crisis maps, relief workers arrive at the locations where they're needed.

_____ People affected by the disaster take photos and send text messages.

_____ This data is used to generate crisis maps.

_____ A disaster, such as an earthquake or a cyclone, strikes.

_____ Relief workers analyze crisis maps.

A rescue worker provides water after an earthquake in Pakistan.

28 **Work in pairs.** According to the video, what role does the TV news play during a crisis? Describe a time when you watched TV news to learn about a crisis. What was happening? What did you see and hear about on TV? How did you respond?

29 **Discuss in groups.** What skills do you have that would help you be an effective crisis mapper?

30 **Choose an activity.**

1. **Work independently.** Research the 2015 Nepal earthquake. What happened? Who helped? How? Write a news report to summarize the story.

2. **Work in pairs.** What is the difference between being a digital and a real-world humanitarian? List at least three differences. Is one more important than the other? More effective? Discuss your opinions.

3. **Work in groups.** At the end of the video, you're told to go online to learn more about crisis mapping organizations. Do this, and take notes on what you find. Prepare a short presentation for your classmates on organizations looking for digital humanitarians and what they need.

Quantifiers: Expressing amounts

Half of/Fifty percent of the world's population **is** . . .

The majority of/Most people are . . .

A number of radio stations **are** online.

A lot of/Two-thirds of/Sixty-seven percent of the people **are** . . .

The majority of/Most of the population **is** . . .

The number of radio stations worldwide **is** 51,000.

31 **Work independently.** Look at the graphic. Use the words below to summarize the information.

1. over half / population / every day

Over half of the world's population listens to the radio every day.

2. majority / farmers / access to radio

_____

_____

3. a lot / young people / Internet

_____

_____

4. percent / population / under 30

_____

_____

5. percent / Africans / under 30

_____

_____

32 **Work in groups.** Make predictions about life in 20 years. Choose a topic and talk about it using an expression of quantity.

In twenty years, 99 percent of students will bring their own computers to school.

Go to p. 157.

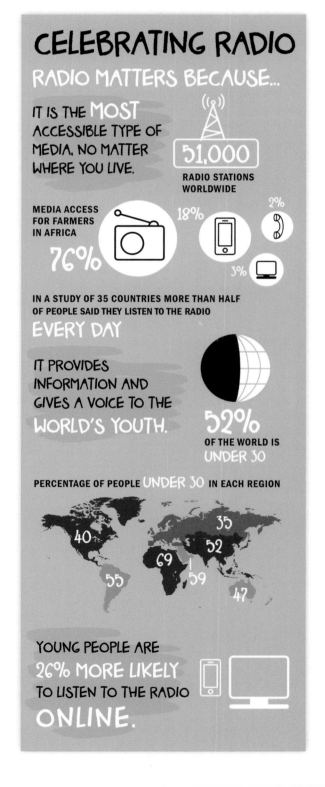

CELEBRATING RADIO

RADIO MATTERS BECAUSE...

IT IS THE MOST ACCESSIBLE TYPE OF MEDIA, NO MATTER WHERE YOU LIVE.

51,000
RADIO STATIONS WORLDWIDE

MEDIA ACCESS FOR FARMERS IN AFRICA
76%
18%
2%
3%

IN A STUDY OF 35 COUNTRIES MORE THAN HALF OF PEOPLE SAID THEY LISTEN TO THE RADIO

EVERY DAY

IT PROVIDES INFORMATION AND GIVES A VOICE TO THE WORLD'S YOUTH.

52%
OF THE WORLD IS UNDER 30

PERCENTAGE OF PEOPLE UNDER 30 IN EACH REGION

40
35
52
69
59
55
47

YOUNG PEOPLE ARE 26% MORE LIKELY TO LISTEN TO THE RADIO ONLINE.

WRITING

In persuasive writing, you express your opinion or point of view about something important to you and support it, using phrases like:

based on   **equally important/necessary**

especially   **It's clear that**

33 **Read the model.** Work in pairs. How does the writer persuade the reader? Underline the words and phrases.

Did you know that February 13 is UNESCO's World Radio Day? On World Radio Day, UNESCO encourages young people to get involved with their local radio stations, get on the air, and even create their own programs. UNESCO believes it is especially important that there be more "Radio for Youth by Youth." This will help young people get connected with one another and learn about the world around them.

More people have access to radio than to TV, computers, or phones. A number of people can only get information on what is happening in the world from the radio. Equally important, there is almost no programming targeting young people, and yet we make up the majority of the population in many parts of the world.

Radio Tumaini, in Dar es Salaam, Tanzania, is one of the few stations that has a youth program. Based on what workers and teen presenters say, the program is a success. Young people are able to use radio to talk about topics that they care about, and listeners especially like hearing the teens tell of their experiences.

It's clear that we need to get involved in radio and make talk shows about issues that are important to us. Let's become reporters and tell the stories we think are important. There is an audience out there, waiting to hear what we have to say.

34 **Work in pairs.** Look again at the graphic on p. 36. What other persuasive information about youth and radio could the writer have included in this paragraph?

35 **Write.** Persuade your readers to take part in a local or global community service project.

Do Your Part

"We're proving what can happen when ordinary people collaborate and use technology to make a positive, lifesaving difference."

—Patrick Meier

National Geographic Explorer, Crisis Mapper

1. **Watch scene 2.2.**

2. Have you ever used technology to help others? Does technology make it more likely that you will do your part when there's a natural disaster? Explain.

3. Patrick Meier uses technology to bring people together from all over the world. How are you using technology now to connect with people around the world? How do you think this will change in the future?

Make an Impact

A **Raise awareness for charity.**

· Research a local or international charity.
· Create a presentation about the charity's mission.
· Present your work to the class.

B **Discover a teen inventor.**

· Choose a teenage inventor who has made something to help others.
· Research their invention and how they made it. Create a drawing of it.
· Explain the invention to the class.

C **Invent a solution yourself.**

· Think of a problem that affects a lot of people.
· Design a technological gadget that could solve this problem.
· Explain to the class how your gadget works.

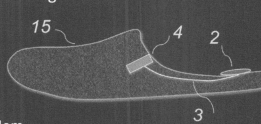

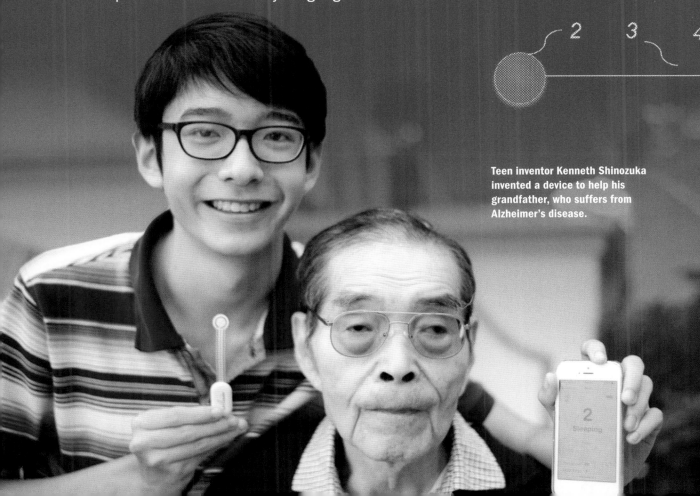

Teen inventor Kenneth Shinozuka invented a device to help his grandfather, who suffers from Alzheimer's disease.

Express Yourself

1 Read and listen to *The Adventures of Crisis Crusher.* TR: 29

The Adventures of Crisis Crusher

IN TIMES OF CRISIS, WHO CAN YOU TURN TO? CRISIS CRUSHER IS ALWAYS THERE TO HELP. BUT WHEN CRISIS CRUSHER IS IN TROUBLE, WHO CAN HE TURN TO?

2 Discuss in groups.

1. What happens in the comic strip?

2. What obstacles do the characters have to overcome?

3. Why does Crisis Crusher need the help of others? How do the people

3 **Connect ideas.** In Unit 1, you learned how people push physical and mental limits to achieve their personal goals. In Unit 2, you learned about people working together for a common goal. In both cases, people overcome obstacles for a purpose. What does this tell you about yourself? What can you accomplish by yourself? What can you accomplish with the help of others?

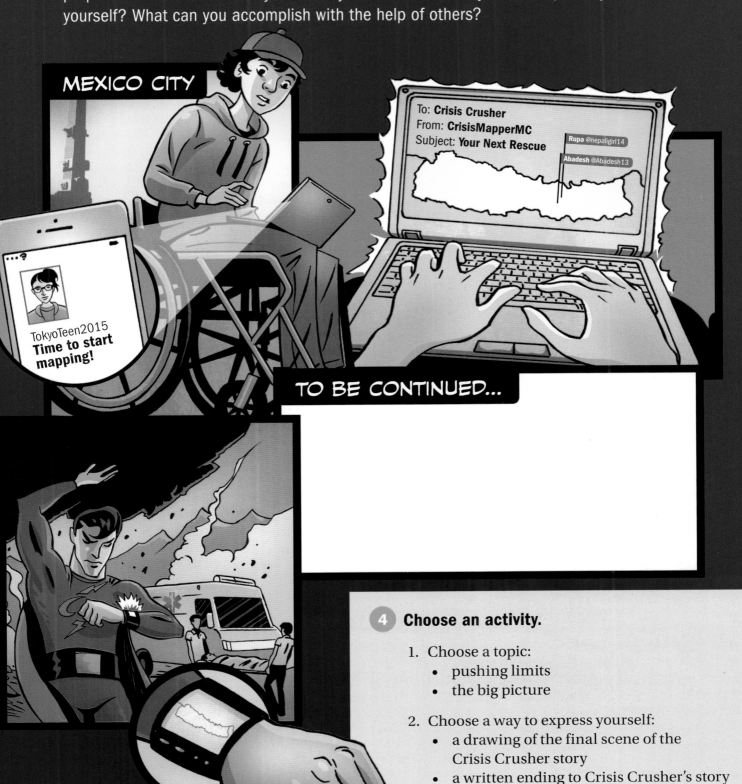

MEXICO CITY

TokyoTeen2015
Time to start mapping!

To: **Crisis Crusher**
From: **CrisisMapperMC**
Subject: **Your Next Rescue**

Rupa @nepaligirl14

Abadesh @Abadesh13

TO BE CONTINUED...

4 **Choose an activity.**

1. Choose a topic:
   - pushing limits
   - the big picture

2. Choose a way to express yourself:
   - a drawing of the final scene of the Crisis Crusher story
   - a written ending to Crisis Crusher's story
   - a theme song for Crisis Crusher

3. Present your work.

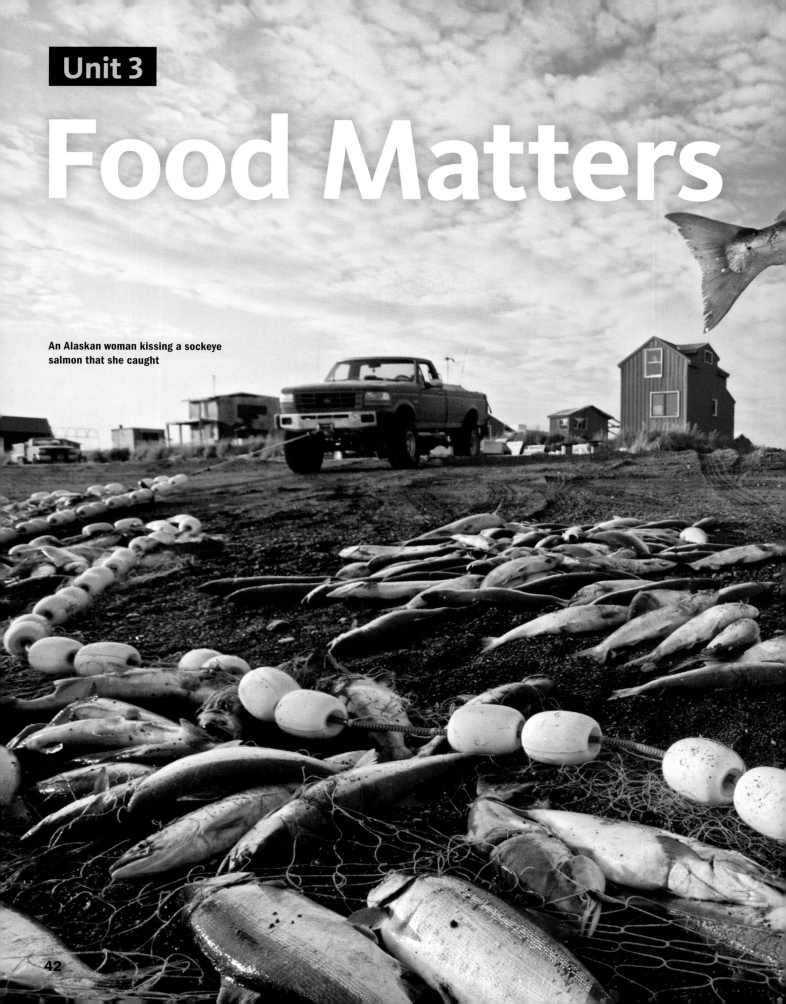

Food Matters

An Alaskan woman kissing a sockeye
salmon that she caught

"As an act of exploration, taste your world."
—Barton Seaver

1. Why do you think this woman is kissing a fish?

2. Why is food important for your health? For your culture? Explain.

3. What are some of your favorite foods? Where do you get these foods?

Modern industrial farming

1 **Where does our food come from? Why does it matter?** Discuss. Then listen and read. TR: 30

What did you eat for breakfast this morning? For dinner last night? You might have mealtime routines that are the same— or almost the same—each day. But did you ever stop and think about the connection you have to food?

In the past, people often grew their own crops and raised their own animals. Once the food was **harvested**, they worked together to get the food to the table. This collaboration helped people to connect with one another, and with the food they prepared.

Harvesting food

Chef and **conservationist** Barton Seaver realized at a young age that food is part of the human experience. As a child, Barton lived in a **diverse** community. Immigrants who lived there brought foods from their cultures with them. Barton's parents cooked with these foods, and Barton was grateful to be able to explore the world right from his kitchen. He learned that food is a **reflection** of culture: it's part of who we are.

Today, this connection between food and people is breaking down. **Globalization** allows food to be shipped anywhere in the world. Since you can buy

according to your **tastes**, there's no need to wait until foods become available. And you don't have to spend hours preparing meals as a family. Foods have been prepared and **packaged** to be more **convenient**. Although they make life easier, these foods are not as **wholesome** as fresh, **local** foods. Packaging and transporting foods also **impacts** the environment.

Barton studies the effects of our food choices on the environment, especially the oceans. He understands that we have preferences about seafood, and that fishermen try to get us what we want. But **commercial** fishing has upset the ocean's ecosystem, and Barton is working to help people change their attitudes about food so that they make better choices.

So, the next time you sit down to a nice entrée of fish and vegetables, think about what you're eating. Are the vegetables from a nearby farm or from across the world? Is the fish on your plate an overfished species? Enjoy your dinner, but don't ignore where it comes from. Remember, your choices count!

2 **Learn new words.** Listen and repeat. TR: 31

3 **Work in pairs.** Describe what you ate and drank at your last meal. Was it wholesome? Where do you think this meal came from? What impact do you think it had on the environment?

4 **Read and write the words from the list.** Make any necessary changes.

commercial	diverse	globalization	harvest	impact
local	packaged	reflection	taste	wholesome

According to Barton, food is a _____ of our culture. He should know. Barton grew up in a very _____ community, where he learned about different cultures through food. Barton sees food as a way to connect with people we know and people we don't know. Trying new foods can _____ our relationship with people, and help us understand other cultures. Barton also sees _____ foods as the best choice. Choosing from what's produced nearby makes us try new things, not just buy according to our _____ . Although _____ farming and fishing offer a wide variety of foods in the supermarket, Barton wants us to avoid popular, overfished species, and instead try the "catch of the day." We should get creative with what is available to create unique, _____ meals.

5 **Learn new words.** Listen for these words and then match them to the correct definition. Then, listen and repeat. TR: 32 and 33

attitude	entrée	grateful

_____ 1. feeling or opinion

_____ 2. main part of a meal

_____ 3. thankful

Commercial fishing

6 **Choose an activity.**

1. **Work independently.** Think about the food produced in your region, and plan an entrée that uses local ingredients. Present your meal idea to the class.
2. **Work in pairs.** Discuss what affects your food choices more: your own tastes or what foods are available to you. Do you make good food choices? Explain.
3. **Work in groups.** Create a survey of food awareness. Work together to write five questions about food. Conduct the survey in class. Then present the results.

Offering advice	Accepting or declining advice
You should think about <u>helping us in the community garden.</u>	Actually, I was thinking <u>we could work at the school's garden.</u>
If I were you, I'd <u>sign up for the school's gardening club.</u>	Great idea! Thanks for the suggestion!
Why don't you try <u>growing vegetables at home?</u>	Thanks for the idea, but I <u>prefer working in my grandfather's garden.</u>

7 **Listen.** How do the speakers offer and respond to advice? Write the words and phrases you hear. TR: 35

8 **Read and complete the dialogue.**

Natalia: I'm so tired of eating the same old thing.

Alex: _____ eating something different? What foods do you like?

Natalia: Well, I love chicken, bread, rice . . .

Alex: _____ , I'd look for dishes from other cultures with those ingredients. Have you tried Indian food?

Natalia: No. _____ , but I don't eat spicy foods.

Alex: Not all Indian food is spicy. And many Indian dishes use chicken and rice. Indian bread, called *naan,* is really delicious, too!

Natalia: Really?

Alex: Really! _____ you could come over and try some Indian food at my house. My dad's making it tomorrow night.

Natalia: _____

9 **Work in groups.** Spin the wheel. Give advice on the topic. Listen as group members respond to your advice.

> You should think about trying sardines. They're really good!

Shopping locally
Eating packaged food
Protecting the environment
Preparing a wholesome entrée
Trying a new food

Go to p. 157.

10 **Work in pairs.** You want to eat more responsibly. Listen and respond to your partner's advice on how to do so.

Mixed conditionals: Expressing how things would be different

If I **hadn't learned** about overfishing, **I would** still **be eating** tuna.

If you **had learned** about Indian food sooner, **you wouldn't** still **be eating** pizza all the time.

11 **Read.** Circle the correct answer.

1. If I *had learned / learned* how to cook, I *wouldn't be / wouldn't have been* eating sandwiches all the time.

2. I *wouldn't have been / wouldn't be* eating chips now, if I *had remembered / remembered* to pack my lunch.

3. What *would we call / would we have called* a sandwich today if the Earl of Sandwich *didn't ask / hadn't asked* for his food to be served between two pieces of toast?

12 **Listen.** Complete the sentences. TR: 37

1. If Barton Seaver hadn't grown up in a family where trying different foods was so important, _____

   _____ .

2. _____ ,

   we would still be more closely connected to what we eat.

3. If we had stayed more connected to our food, _____

   _____ .

13 **Work in pairs.** Talk about what would be different now in these situations.

1. If I had never tried (food), . . .

2. If I had (never) learned to cook, . . .

3. If I hadn't learned about food awareness, . . .

> If I had learned to cook when I was younger, I wouldn't be eating so much packaged food.

> Yeah, and if I hadn't learned about food awareness, I wouldn't read labels carefully.

14 **Learn new words.** Listen and read about food revolutionaries. Then listen and repeat. **TR: 38 and 39**

Barton Seaver

Christopher Columbus (1451–1506)

Auguste Escoffier (1846–1935)

You have already learned that Barton Seaver is a food **revolutionary**. He wants to change the way we eat, especially seafood. According to Barton, if we hadn't overfished popular fishes like tuna and cod, the ocean's ecosystem wouldn't be out of balance. Barton understands that fish is in demand because it's a healthy source of **protein**. He just wants people to try fish that are lower on the food chain. This would help **restore** the population of overfished species. Barton is trying to make changes today, but there were other food revolutionaries long before him.

Christopher Columbus is known around the world as an explorer. But Columbus is also one of the first food revolutionaries. If he hadn't traveled west in search of **spices** from India, he would have never arrived in the Americas. And if he and other explorers hadn't arrived in the Americas, foods such as tomatoes, potatoes, corn, and cacao would not have been brought back to Europe. Without Columbus's exploration, the modern diet of many cultures would be much different.

Another food revolutionary is French chef Auguste Escoffier. Escoffier wanted to make the process of cooking more standard. He wrote down ingredients and necessary steps for each of his dishes. If Escoffier hadn't done this, we might not have **recipes** or cookbooks!

15 **Work in pairs.** Talk about how things would be if it weren't for food revolutionaries. Used mixed conditionals in your discussion, as well as the words from the box.

corn	fish	potato	recipe	spice	write

16 **Work independently.** Research another food revolutionary, such as Julia Child, Clarence Birdseye, or Ettore Boiardi. Write about the person you chose. Tell how things would be different if it hadn't been for that person's work. Present your research to the class.

Tomatoes and corn were brought to Europe from the Americas in the 1500s.

National Geographic Explorer Caleb Harper and his CityFarm

Grow
IT HERE,
Eat
IT HERE

With 80 percent of the world's population living in cities by the year 2050, we need to consider indoor farming.

What do you think of when you hear the word *farm*? You probably think of a large, open land with lots of different crops growing and animals grazing, right? Well, urban agriculturalist Caleb Harper is working to

Over the past few years, Caleb has been researching different forms of vertical farming. He has been working to bring farms into the city. His main focus is on two types of vertical farming: *aeroponics* and *hydroponics*. With aeroponics, a nutrient-filled mist is sprayed on a plant's roots to help them grow without soil. With hydroponics, a plant is grown in nutrient-rich water.

Caleb uses simple computer technologies to monitor his crops. This technology allows him to control climate and provide consistent light, food, temperature, and water. The result is better plant growth and flavor. This consistency also allows his crops to produce food four to five times faster than those of a traditional outdoor farmer.

Caleb's work is important. Right now, we are facing a global food crisis. The world's population is at 7 billion. In 30 years, it will be nearly 9 billion. We will need to produce 70 percent more food to feed these additional people, but there isn't enough farmland.

Even if there were, traditional farming can be harmful to land. Overused soil loses nutrients. Farmers use chemicals to treat their crops. These chemicals get into the ground and run off into bodies of water. The polluted water supply threatens the ecosystem and the health of those living nearby.

Vertical farming systems can help solve these problems. First, farms in urban areas will allow people to harvest fresh produce year-round. There is no need to worry about threats such as droughts or insects, which could ruin a crop. And indoor farms are sustainable. They use less water than a traditional farm, and with aeroponics, 97 percent of fresh water is reused. Vertical farms use less energy because they don't depend on large farming equipment and long transportation systems to carry the food from farm to city. And all of the crops in an indoor farm are grown without pesticides, so they are fresh, healthy, and organic.

So, the next time you hear the word *farm*, don't just think of that large, open land with crops and animals. Think inside the city—it's the future of farming.

20 **After you read, work in pairs to answer the questions.**

1. Describe Caleb Harper's indoor farm.
2. Why is Caleb's work important?
3. What are *aeroponics* and *hydroponics*?
4. What are two problems with traditional farming?
5. What are three ways that indoor farms are sustainable?

21 **Work in groups.** Using what you learned in the unit, discuss whether you think Barton Seaver would support Caleb's work. Give examples to support your ideas.

22 **Discuss in groups.**

1. Vertical farms will help provide food for our growing population. What is another way we can produce more food?

2. Apart from the health and environmental benefits, what other benefits could indoor farming bring to a city?

51

VIDEO ▶

A plate of *chapulines*

23 Before you watch, discuss in groups.

1. What is the most unusual food you have ever eaten? Why did you try it? Did you like it?

2. Look at the photo of *chapulines*. This dish is eaten in parts of Mexico. Have you ever tried this dish, or a similar one? Would you try it? Why or why not?

24 Work in pairs. The video presents problems related to food, and how eating insects might solve those problems. Predict a problem and a solution that the video may mention. Write your answers in the space below.

Problem	Solution
_____	_____
_____	_____
_____	_____

25 Watch scene 3.1. While you watch, check your predictions from Activity 24.

A grasshopper

26 **After you watch, read the sentences below.** Use the information from the video to decide if each one is *true* or *false*.

1. Presently, very few people in the world eat insects. Ⓣ Ⓕ

2. Beetles and caterpillars are the insects most commonly eaten by people. Ⓣ Ⓕ

3. There are fewer than 200 species of edible insects. Ⓣ Ⓕ

4. Insects are a good solution to the increased demand for protein. Ⓣ Ⓕ

5. Insects are already being used to produce food for farm animals. Ⓣ Ⓕ

6. Eating insects is really harmful for the environment. Ⓣ Ⓕ

27 **Work in pairs.** This video suggests that we try something new, even if it seems unpleasant. Think about a time when you had to try a new dish, even though you didn't want to. Who or what made you try it? Was it what you expected? Explain.

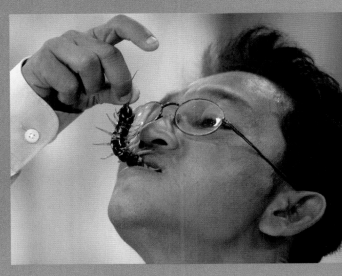

Eating a centipede

28 **Choose an activity.**

1. **Work independently.** Find out about another unusual food source that people may not want to eat, such as snake meat or snails. Learn about where this food is eaten, who eats it, and how it is prepared. Write a paragraph to summarize what you learned.

2. **Work in pairs**. Make a list of six things that people would consider unpleasant to eat, such as insects, worms, or certain animal parts. Survey ten people to find out which of these things they are most likely to try, and which they wouldn't try. Present your survey results to the class.

3. **Work in groups.** Prepare a radio commercial to convince listeners to try eating insects. In your commercial, explain at least three benefits of eating insects.

Double comparatives: Describing outcomes

The more people there are in the world, **the more** food we need to produce.

The less our food travels, **the less** it impacts the environment.

The more we choose wholesome foods, **the healthier** we are.

The less we eat processed foods, **the better**.

29 **Complete the sentences with comparative phrases.**

1. The more new foods we try, _____ .

2. The less time we spend cooking, _____ .

3. The more we know about food, _____ .

4. The less we waste food, _____ .

5. The more indoor farms there are, _____ .

6. The higher the population, _____ .

7. The less we use chemicals, _____ .

8. The more seafood we demand, _____ .

30 **Work in pairs.** Discuss two ways that food choices impact the environment. Use comparative sentences in your discussion.

> The more we ship food across the world, the more we impact the environment.

> That's right! And the more we buy from local farms, the less we impact the environment.

31 **Work in groups.** Take a card. Use a comparative sentence to comment on the topic. Then, discuss the comment. Each group member should agree or disagree with the comment.

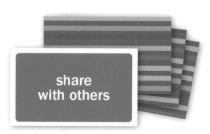

share with others

Go to p. 159.

54

WRITING

When you write a review, you combine facts and opinions to describe a place (such as a hotel or a restaurant) or a thing (such as a book, a song, or a movie). Use the following words to show your attitude when writing a review:

actually   **clearly**   **honestly**   **more/most importantly**   **(un)fortunately**

32 **Read the model.** Work in pairs to identify the facts, and the author's opinions about the restaurant. What words does the writer use when showing his/her attitude about the restaurant? Underline the words.

If you are looking for a great meal, you should really go to Jozsa's Restaurant. The more I eat there, the better it gets. I'm not the only one who thinks that Jozsa's has the best food in town: the restaurant has actually won many awards for its excellent dishes, such as roasted chicken with potatoes and beef with noodles. The fish entrées are all delicious as well. Everything at this restaurant is worth a try. And don't forget to save room for dessert. Honestly, the chocolate cake is the best you'll ever have!

Clearly, the chef at this restaurant uses fresh ingredients. There is a large garden behind the restaurant where they grow vegetables and herbs that are used in the dishes. Nothing on the menu is made with packaged foods. For this reason, I feel like Jozsa's is a great choice for a wholesome meal if you can't cook at home.

Fortunately, Jozsa's is open every night from 5:00 to 11:00, and for lunch on the weekends. The restaurant is very busy, so you will want to make a reservation. The service is fantastic every time! The workers are friendly, and more importantly, they always have the food on your table quickly. The inside and outside of the restaurant are both great places to eat. If it's cold outside, try to get a seat next to the fireplace. In nice weather, you can enjoy your dinner in the garden.

Every time my family has something to celebrate, we choose Jozsa's. If you haven't tried Jozsa's yet, you don't know what you're missing!

33 **Work in pairs.** Does this review convince you to try this restaurant? Why or why not?

34 **Write.** Write a review of your favorite restaurant. Give both facts and opinions about the food, the service, and the surroundings.

Know Your Food

"Take some time to educate yourself about the right decisions—and make a difference in the health of the planet."

—Barton Seaver

National Geographic Explorer, Chef/Conservationist

1. Watch scene 3.2.

2. How much do you know about the food that you eat each day? Why is it important to be informed about food choices?

3. What steps can you take to learn more about the food you eat? Name at least two things you can do to be better informed.

Make an Impact

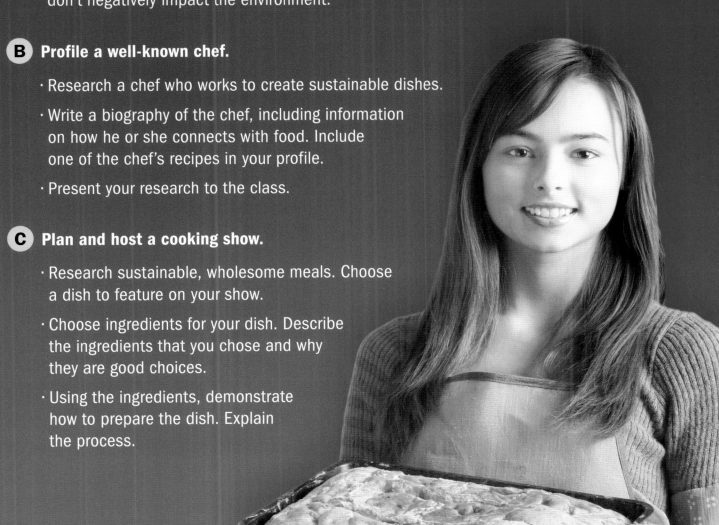

A **Create a sustainable lunch menu.**

· List food groups that you would include on a lunch menu.

· Research sustainable options for each of these food groups.

· Create a lunch menu for a week that includes wholesome foods that don't negatively impact the environment.

B **Profile a well-known chef.**

· Research a chef who works to create sustainable dishes.

· Write a biography of the chef, including information on how he or she connects with food. Include one of the chef's recipes in your profile.

· Present your research to the class.

C **Plan and host a cooking show.**

· Research sustainable, wholesome meals. Choose a dish to feature on your show.

· Choose ingredients for your dish. Describe the ingredients that you chose and why they are good choices.

· Using the ingredients, demonstrate how to prepare the dish. Explain the process.

The Footprint of Fun

"An individual action, multiplied by millions, creates global change."
—Jack Johnson

Japanese fans wave trash bags before cleaning up after a World Cup game.

1. When you attend a sporting event, do you clean up after yourself? Why or why not?

2. What fun things can you think of that might not be good for the environment? Which of them do you do?

3. What do you like to do for fun that doesn't harm the environment?

Tivoli Gardens in Copenhagen, Denmark

Your last visit to an **amusement** park was probably pretty **enjoyable**, wasn't it? **Attractions** such as rides, shows, and games are really fun for visitors. While you're on a roller coaster or playing games in the arcade, you probably don't consider your environmental impact.

Think about it: Amusement parks **consume** huge amounts of energy. Just going up the hill of one roller coaster ride uses enough energy to power a lamp for over 30 hours. Some high-speed rides use enough energy to power a small town. Amusement parks also use **excessive** amounts of water in rides, fountains, and other park **facilities**. And then there is the issue of garbage. Tons of **litter** are being produced in amusement parks by the millions of people who visit. Disneyland alone produces over 300,000 tons of litter each year, more than a mid-sized city!

Parks such as Ancol Dreamland in Jakarta, Indonesia, have recycling programs for visitors.

Conservation is nothing new for the **industry**. Walt Disney thought about it back in 1955 while designing his first park, Disneyland California. Disney himself planned for the use of recycled water throughout his park. Even today, employees of Disney's parks are proactive in keeping them sustainable. At Disneyland Hong Kong, run-off rainwater is being collected into a lake and then reused throughout the resort. And Disney parks are designed to be clean, with trash cans located every 30 steps inside the park. Each one leads to an underground system where trash is pushed through pipes at over 95 kph (60 mph) and ultimately compacted. Disney is also taking action to prevent waste. By using recyclable materials and **composting**, the parks have reduced trash by over 60 percent.

Other parks are also becoming **sensitive** of their environmental impact. They are starting to **participate** in the green **movement** with positive **results**. Park vehicles and trains at the US-based Six Flags, now run on used vegetable oil from the parks' kitchens. Copenhagen's Tivoli Gardens, one of the oldest amusement parks in the world, has a windmill that generates all its electricity.

These changes produce both environmental and **economic** benefits. As sustainable ideas and technology become more **accessible**, it's easier than ever for amusement parks to be green!

2 **Learn new words.** Listen and repeat. TR: 44

3 **Work in pairs.** Describe a recent trip to an amusement park or a public event. Did you see any litter there? Was there an effort to recycle? What else was being done to protect the environment?

4 **Read and write the words from the list.** Make any necessary changes.

accessible	consume	economic	enjoyable	excessive
industry	litter	participate	result	sensitive

It's good to know that the music _____ has environmental champions like Jack Johnson. Jack is a singer and surfer who is very _____ about nature. He was concerned about the negative impact his concert tours were having on the environment. So he decided to cut out _____ waste and _____ less energy. The _____ of that decision is that Jack now fuels his tour buses with biofuel, and performs at places that are _____ by public transportation. He also invites nonprofits to _____ in educating fans about sustainability at his concert venues.

Jack Johnson

5 **Learn new words.** Listen for these words and match them to the definitions. Then listen and repeat. **TR: 45 and 46**

benefit	nonprofit	proactive	to take action

_____ 1. a positive effect

_____ 2. preparing for possible future problems

_____ 3. do something about a problem

_____ 4. an organization not focused on making money

6 **Choose an activity.**

1. **Work independently.** Research what another well-known person or organization is doing for the environment. Share what you learned with the class.

2. **Work in pairs.** Keep a journal of what you throw in the trash in a day. Compare with your partner. How much waste did you produce? How can you reduce the amount of waste you produce?

3. **Work in groups.** Do you think musicians should be responsible for making their events more environmentally friendly? What can they say or do to make their fans more proactive in protecting the planet? Discuss. Then list three suggestions.

Defending your opinion

I heard that <u>race cars really use a lot of fuel</u>.

I read that <u>they use around 20,000 l (5,300 gal.) in a race</u>.

Most people would agree that <u>there are greener forms of entertainment</u>.

As far as I know, <u>these industries are trying to go green</u>.

All I'm saying is <u>that electric cars and airplanes will change the industry</u>.

7 **Listen.** How do the speakers defend their opinions? Write the phrases you hear. **TR: 48**

8 **Read and complete the dialogue.**

Jakub: Hey, Lille. My family and I are going to the air show on Saturday. Would you like to join us?

Lille: Well, air shows are a little too noisy for me. _____ they're really bad for the environment, too.

Jakub: Well, it's true that air shows do consume a lot of fuel. But, _____ , the industry is developing new, more efficient planes. _____ an electric plane might fly all the way around the world.

Lille: Right, but the planes at the show won't be electric. Those planes burn a lot of fuel *and* blow smoke into the environment. _____ they have a huge environmental impact.

Jakub: Actually, _____ the colored smoke is biodegradable and doesn't harm the environment.

Lille: Well, the fuel that's burned certainly does. Sorry, Jakub. I hope you have fun, but I would rather not come. Let's get together Sunday instead. You can tell me all about the show.

9 **Work in pairs.** Take turns giving and defending your opinion using the information on the cards.

Buying bottled water isn't bad for the environment. You just need to recycle the bottles.

Really? I've heard that only 1 in 5 bottles actually gets recycled.

10 **Work in groups.** Discuss the information on the cards again. This time, express your own opinion.

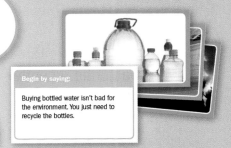

Begin by saying:

Buying bottled water isn't bad for the environment. You just need to recycle the bottles.

Go to p. 161.

63

Passives: Describing actions and processes

What have musicians done to reduce their ecological footprint?	What **has been done** by musicians to reduce their ecological footprint?
Jack Johnson's music is promoting sustainability.	Sustainability **is being promoted** through Jack Johnson's music.
Jack can teach his fans about conservation. They will pass on the ideas to their friends.	Jack's fans **can be taught** about conservation. The ideas **will be passed on** to friends.

11 **Read the information in the graphic.** Underline the examples of the passive.

12 **Listen. Complete the sentences.** TR: 50

So you _____ that some fun activities can harm the environment. But Jack Johnson is working toward his goal that the environment _____ by his concerts. Water refill stations _____ throughout his concert venues. Fans _____ to bring their own reusable water bottles. And Jack's team works together with local farms to make sure that sustainable food _____ . Jack hopes that his message is coming through, and that his fans _____ by their experience at his show.

13 **Work in groups.** Talk about environmental improvements to your school or city. What has been done to protect the environment? What was done recently? What else can be done? What do you think will be done in the near future? Use the passive in your discussion.

200 BILLION LITERS (53 billion gal.) of bottled water are being consumed worldwide every year.

More than **40%** of all bottled water is being produced from **TAP WATER.**

Bottled water can be sold at nearly **10,000** TIMES the price of tap water.

Bottled water has **NOT** been found to be **SAFER** than tap water.

Almost **1/4** of bottled water has been **CONTAMINATED.**

Only **1** IN **5** water bottles is being recycled.

More than **1** MILLION METRIC TONS (3 BILLION LB.) of waste will be produced from the other four bottles.

14 **Learn new words.** Read about the effects of plastic on the environment, and what you can do about it. Then listen and repeat. **TR: 51 and 52**

Recently, the worldwide **demand** for plastic has exploded. Plastic is all around us—our gadgets, dishes, furniture—almost everything is made of plastic these days! Plastic is convenient, but most of us never think about the **damage** caused by using too much plastic.

Jack says, "**Challenge** yourself to reduce your plastic footprint."

Why should we do this? And how can we?

Litter from plastic products dirties our cities. Much of the plastic ends up in landfills, where it can last up to 500 years! But worse is that our oceans are being polluted by plastics. There are around 8 million tons of plastic **waste** in the world's oceans. Over 700 species of marine wildlife have been **harmed** by this pollution. Many animals mistake plastic for food. Over 100,000 marine animals die each year from eating plastic. Others might survive, but some of them end up on our plates. So, humans are also being harmed by plastic in the oceans.

To make a positive change, we can:

- Reduce the amount of plastic we use each day.
- Reuse by carrying our own water bottles and bags.
- Recycle any additional plastic we use.

Whether you're going to school, to the park, or to a concert, think about your footprint.

A sea turtle tries to eat a plastic bag that it has mistaken for a jellyfish.

15 **Work in pairs.** Think about Jack's message. Write five things that can be done to reduce the use of plastic in your daily life. Use the passive.

16 **Work in groups.** Research how bottled water consumption and recycling have changed over the years. Present what you learned to the class, using the passive.

> Ten percent more bottled water is being consumed each year.

17 **Before you read, discuss in pairs.**
Based on what you learned so far in this unit and the photos on this page, what do you think the reading is about?

18 **Learn new words.** Find these words in the reading. What do you think they mean? Use the other words in the sentence to help you. Then listen and repeat. TR: 53

| cost | development | to maintain | venue |

19 **While you read, think about the author's purpose.** TR: 54

20 **After you read, work in pairs to answer the questions.**

1. What is a benefit of hosting the Olympics?
2. What are two negative results of hosting the Olympics?
3. What was the total cost of the 2004 Summer Olympics?
4. Give an example of how an Olympic site is being reused.
5. What should Olympic host cities do to avoid ending up with a "ghost town"?

GAME OVER

After the torch goes out, what happens to Olympic sites?

How would you feel if your city were chosen to host the Olympic Games? The best athletes in the world would be right outside your door! The games bring excitement and attention to your region, as well as a lot of development. But the Olympics also have great economic and environmental costs. People have even been forced to leave their homes to make way for the Olympics. And once the last medal is awarded and the athletes have gone home, you may be left with a ghost town.

Greece is the birthplace of the Olympics. So the country was excited to welcome the 2004 Summer Olympics back to Athens.

An abandoned Olympic training pool in Athens, Greece

After years of preparation, and nearly $11 billion spent, the athletes arrived, and the games began. The 2004 Summer Olympics were a success. But shortly after they ended, the venues began to fall apart. Most of them sit empty today. The Olympic training pool is used by frogs, not athletes. Until recently, the Greek government was still paying to maintain these buildings, bringing the total cost of the 2004 Summer Olympics to over $50 billion. Athens isn't alone. Many Olympic sites have become ghost towns. The abandoned site of the 1936 Summer Olympics is still standing in Berlin, nearly a century after it was built.

With good planning, Olympic venues can be successfully reused. In many cities, former Olympic stadiums continue to host sporting events. Barcelona, host of the 1992 Summer Olympics, has been creative in reusing its venues. Barcelona's Port Olímpic, built for the Olympic sailing competition, is now a popular tourist destination, with a museum, hotels, shops, and restaurants. Tourists visiting Beijing can now enjoy a water park experience at the Water Cube, where swimming records were broken during the 2008 Summer Olympics.

Hosting the Olympic Games is an honor. But the games only last seventeen days! Olympic venues shouldn't simply be designed to be used for a couple of weeks. These facilities can improve a region only when they're designed for the long-term benefit of everyone. Architects who create quality facilities that serve a community for the years after the Olympics deserve a gold medal!

The Water Cube in Beijing, China

21 **Work in pairs.** Think about the information in the reading. Why do you think the author wrote this text? What is the author's message?

22 **Discuss in groups.**

1. Would you like the Olympics to come to your country? Why or why not?

2. Imagine your city or town has been chosen to host the Olympic Games. What needs to be built? How will your city change?

3. What could the International Olympic Committee do to make sure that the venues designed for the Olympic Games don't turn into "ghost towns"? Give two or three examples.

3 **Before you watch, discuss in groups.** Describe the size and the atmosphere of a concert or big sporting event that you've attended.

4 **Before you watch, discuss in groups.** You're going to watch a video called *The Footprint of Fans.* Based on what you learned so far in this unit, predict three ways fans leave an ecological footprint when they attend an event.

5 Watch scene 4.1. **While you watch, fill in a T-chart.** List two problems and two solutions mentioned in the video.

6 **After you watch, complete the sentences below.**

1. Fans are responsible for up to

   _____ of a concert's carbon footprint.

2. Some concert venues reward fans who carpool by giving them _____ .

3. Some sporting events can fill a stadium with

   up to _____ fans.

4. Sports fans can leave behind

   _____ tons of waste.

5. Recycled plastic and other materials are now

   used to make _____ .

Fans at the closing ceremony for the 2015 European Games held in Baku, Azerbaijan.

27 **Work in pairs.** Check the ways the video suggests that we can reduce our fan footprint.

- ☐ only watch games on TV
- ☐ carpool to concerts
- ☐ buy recycled sporting equipment
- ☐ pay less money for tickets
- ☐ recycle water bottles
- ☐ go to fewer concerts and sporting events

28 **Discuss in groups.** Answer the questions you see at the end of the video: *What else are you a fan of? How does it impact the environment? How can you take action to become an eco-friendly fan?*

29 **Choose an activity.**

1. **Work independently.** Research a concert or sporting event. How could the organizers have made the event greener? Write a letter to the organizers presenting at least three ideas.

2. **Work in pairs.** Survey your classmates to find out how many attend big events such as concerts or sporting events. Create five questions about transportation, garbage, energy use, and recycling at these events. Summarize and report your findings.

3. **Work in groups.** Make a short presentation to your local politicians suggesting how to reduce the carbon footprint of big events in your city.

Verbs followed by gerunds or infinitives

Most water parks **want to use less** water.

Park employees **encourage** visitors **to keep** water inside the pool.

We should **stop to look at** the root of the problem.

How can they **avoid wasting** water?

Maybe parks should just **stop using** so much water.

Parks must **continue coming up with / to come up with** ways to reuse water.

30 **Work independently.** Complete the sentences with the correct form of the verb in parentheses. Go to p. 152.

1. This summer, I hope _____ (visit) my favorite water park.

2. Although I can't wait _____ (play) in the water each summer, I agree that parks should start _____ (conserve) more water.

3. Park designers should stop _____ (think) of new ways to use less water.

4. Park operators shouldn't stop _____ (clean) and _____ (reuse) the water in their attractions.

5. Some parks even choose _____ (collect) rainwater for use in their attractions.

6. Of course, if you want _____ (enjoy) water in a way that doesn't harm the environment, consider _____ (go) to the beach!

31 **Work in pairs.** Your school wants students to conserve water. Make a list of five suggestions. Use some of the verbs below followed by an infinitive or a gerund.

ask	avoid	choose	continue	start	stop	tell	want

32 **Work in groups.** You are planning an event to raise awareness for the environment. Toss a coin and take turns moving. (Heads = 1 space; Tails = 2 spaces) Say what you need to do.

> We should think about finding a venue that's accessible by bus.

START

Find a venue that's accessible by bus. (think about)

Advertise with social media, not paper. (continue)

Go to p. 163.

When writing a problem and solution essay, focus on including both information and reflection. Information can be provided about a problem, and reflection on the problem can lead to solutions. When writing about problems and solutions, the following phrases are useful:

Problem:	**due to**	**it's true that**	**the issue is**
Solution:	**in order to**	**one solution is**	**will result in**

33 **Read the model.** What is the problem? Underline the phrases that help you find it.

I love going to water parks for fun. However, many people think that water parks are bad for the environment. The issue is that the parks waste water. Due to a lack of drinking water in many parts of the world, people think water shouldn't be used just to have fun. It's true that thousands of liters of water are used every day at a single water park. And there are nearly 2,000 water parks around the world, so that's a lot of water!

Water park operators understand that they need to conserve water, especially in places with dry climates. One solution that has been developed is to recycle water. Using special filters, water parks are able to clean and reuse most of the water in their facilities. Some indoor water parks are able to recycle as much as 97 percent of the water they use. Outdoor water parks lose water because of the sun. Building attractions in the shade will result in less water being lost. All water parks lose water when visitors splash it out of the pool. So new designs are being created in order to keep water in the pools and prevent it from being wasted.

Water parks attract millions of people each year, so they aren't going away any time soon. If you think water is wasted at water parks, think about how much more water would be used if each visitor instead cooled off with a pool or a sprinkler at home! In that case, you could argue that water parks actually help conserve water.

34 **Work in pairs.** How many solutions did the writer give to the problem? What were they? Think of another solution to the problem.

35 **Write.** Think about an activity that you enjoy that may be harmful to the environment. Write an essay to describe why it's a problem. Give at least three possible solutions to the problem.

Reduce your Footprint

"Your actions, your voice and your choices all have a huge impact."

—Jack Johnson
National Geographic Ambassador to the Arts, Musician

1. Watch scene 4.2.

2. Are you aware of how your actions affect the environment? What are some things you could do to further reduce your footprint?

3. What advice could you offer to friends and family for having fun without harming the environment?

Make an Impact

A **Make an ad promoting clean fun.**

- Brainstorm ways to have fun that don't harm the environment.
- Plan and write a script for an ad that promotes environmentally friendly fun.
- Film your ad and show it to the class.

B **Make a song about the environment.**

- Brainstorm some environmental topics that matter to you.
- Write your lyrics and add music.
- Perform your song!

C **Reduce the footprint of fun at your school.**

- Choose an upcoming event at your school.
- Develop a plan to reduce trash produced at the event.
- Make posters or fliers to promote your ideas.

Express Yourself

1 **Read and listen to the online invitation.** TR: 56

REDUCE,

Inbox>

From: events@impactcommunityschool.edu

To: friends@impactcommunityschool.edu

Subject: **Invitation to our fundraising concert: Reduce, reuse, recycle, rock!**

It's that time of year again when we all come together for our annual fundraiser concert. Last year's event was a huge success, but this year will be even better because it will be completely green! We want to have fun and raise money, but we also want to keep our footprint small. Big changes are being made to achieve that goal. Click on the invitation to learn more. Hope to see you there!

VIEW INVITATION →

REUSE, RECYCLE, ROCK!

WHEN: April 22 at 3:00 P.M.

WHERE: Impact Park

COST: $15.00 in advance,
$20.00 at the event

(Remember, all of the money raised benefits Impact Community School!)

We're reducing our festival footprint by:

- using biofuel tour buses for band transportation
- powering lights with solar energy
- offering only local organic food options
- providing compostable plates and utensils

You can reduce your festival footprint by:

- not printing this invitation
- bringing your own refillable water bottle
- walking, biking, or carpooling to the venue
- forwarding this invitation to a friend

2 **Discuss in groups.**

1. Does the invitation make you want to attend the festival? Why or why not?

2. Name two other ways that the festival organizers could help guests reduce their footprint of fun.

3 **Connect ideas.** In Unit 3, you learned about sustainable eating. In Unit 4, you earned about having fun responsibly. What connection do you see between the two units?

4 **Choose an activity.**

1. Choose a topic:
   - sustainable fun
   - sustainable food

2. Choose a way to express yourself:
   - an online invitation
   - a slideshow
   - a poster

3. Present your work.

Why We Explore

Austrian BASE jumper Felix Baumgartner jumps from the edge of space, 39 km (24 mi.) above the surface of the Earth.

"We really need to show people the world in a different light, in a new format—something that they can engage with and be excited about."
—Corey Jaskolski

1. In the photo, we see a man jump from the edge of space and then free-fall, attached only to a helium balloon. Would you try this? Why or why not?

2. Why do you think people explore? What can be learned from exploring new places?

3. Where would you like to explore? Explain.

The desire for **knowledge** about our world pushes explorers into the smallest caves, the deepest oceans, and even outer space. People have been exploring for centuries. But any explorer will tell you that the more they **investigate**, the more they realize there's still so much to learn.

Explorer Sylvia Earle is a deep-ocean **pioneer** with a long list of achievements. She has engaged in 7,000 hours of underwater study and written nearly 200 scientific articles on her findings. In 1970, she and a team of women "aquanauts" were required to live underwater for weeks at a time to **research** marine life. The fact that so much of the ocean remains undiscovered **has driven** Sylvia's work. In fact, even though explorers have been studying the world's oceans for years, they've only seen about five percent of them! Sylvia's **purpose** in life has been to protect the sea, and she encourages others to do so as well.

Paleoanthropologist Lee Berger has been searching for ancient hominids in **remote** parts of Africa for over two decades. He is **curious** about the family of primates that evolved into *Homo sapiens*, or human beings. Lee has made some **exciting** discoveries over time, but his most important discovery came in 2014 when he led an expedition at the Rising Star cave system, near Johannesburg, South Africa. To explore one of the caves, researchers had to squeeze through an opening less than 25 cm (10 in.) wide. Lee wasn't small enough to do it himself, so he gathered an **expert** team of female researchers who made it inside. There they found over 1,550 bones, representing at least 15 individuals.

The bones were brought to the lab where skeletons were assembled. Lee used 3D scanning to identify an entirely new hominid species: *Homo naledi*. Creating the skeleton was just the first step in understanding the new species. "The discoveries we're now making show that, in some ways, the age of exploration is still just beginning," says Lee.

Engineer and inventor Corey Jaskolski not only explores, but also creates **high-tech** tools that allow people to **look into** the past without harming its artifacts. Corey wants explorers to protect what they **encounter** so that future generations can learn from them, too. "When we discover things, we have a responsibility to preserve them as well," he says.

Scientists working inside the Rising Star cave, where fossils of *Homo naledi* were discovered

2 **Learn new words.** Listen and repeat. TR: 58

3 **Work in pairs.** Why do you think each explorer's contributions are important? How does an explorer's work matter to all of us?

4 **Read and write the words from the list.** Make any necessary changes.

curious	drive	encounter	exciting	expert
high-tech	investigate	knowledge	purpose	remote

Corey Jaskolski is an _____ engineer and inventor whose _____ inventions are helping explorers—and ordinary people—to see the world in a different way. For example, his underwater robotic cameras can get high-resolution photos of very _____ parts of the ocean. These devices were used to _____ and film the *Titanic* shipwreck. Corey has also developed 360-degree viewers for the _____ of allowing people to explore _____ places, such as King Tut's tomb, just by moving their mobile devices! Corey also has created night-vision cameras and 3D camera traps that help photographers capture images of animals without disturbing them. Conservation is what _____ much of Corey's work. His equipment can be used to gain _____ about places or animals without harming them at all. Corey wants to protect what's here on Earth so that future generations can enjoy exploring just like he does.

5 **Learn new words.** Listen for these words and match them to the definitions. Then listen and repeat. TR: 59 and 60

achievement	to encourage	to engage in	to require

Corey Jaskolski

_____ 1. help or support someone

_____ 2. make someone do something

_____ 3. be involved in a cause

_____ 4. success

6 **Choose an activity.**

1. **Work independently.** How well do you know your community? Investigate your area. Explore both online and "in the field." Share your experience with the class.

2. **Work in pairs.** How might technology help in making new discoveries? Make a list of five ideas. Present your list to the class.

3. **Work in groups.** Investigate Corey's work. Which of his inventions would you like to own? What would you do with it?

Hesitating or buying time when answering questions

Where do you see yourself in 5 years?	Hmm . . . that's tough. <u>I'd like to be studying in South America, but I might need to get a job.</u>
What made you want to learn Cantonese?	Well, it's hard to explain. I guess <u>I've just always wanted to travel to Guangzhou.</u>
Why do you think humans explore?	That's a good question. Let me think about that one for a minute.

7 **Listen.** How does the speaker buy time before responding to the question? Write the phrases you hear. **TR: 62**

8 **Read and complete the dialogue.**

Caleb: So Kenji, how do you like living in Canada?

Kenji: _____ I guess I'm enjoying my experience overall, but there have been some challenges.

Caleb: What's been the biggest challenge?

Kenji: _____ . . . probably speaking English all the time and trying to make friends.

Caleb: But joining the baseball team has made you pretty popular. We're number one in the league for the first time! How'd you get so good at it?

Kenji: _____ In Japan, I'm just a normal player. We practice a lot. All year, in fact. Don't you do the same with hockey?

Caleb: Some people do, but I just play for fun. Besides, I like playing baseball in spring.

Kenji: Would you like to visit Japan someday?

Caleb: _____ it'd be fun, but it sounds like I better get serious about baseball first!

9 **Work in pairs.** Cut out the cards on p. 165. Take turns asking each other the questions on the cards. Use the phrases above to buy time when necessary.

> Hmm . . . that's a good question. I'd really like to go to Borneo.

> If you could go anywhere in the world, where would you go?

10 **Work in groups.** Write five original questions to ask your group. Then take turns asking and answering your questions.

> What is your favorite book?

> Hmm . . . that's a tough one. Let me think about that.

Go to p. 165.

11 **Listen.** Answer the questions below using the narrative tenses. TR: 64

1. What happened when Barrington met a Jamaican pilot?

   _____

2. What career had Barrington been preparing for?

   _____

3. How did he start learning to fly?

   _____

4. What had he been offered? Did he accept the offer?

   _____

5. What was Barrington doing before his first solo flight?

   _____

6. How was his first solo flight?

   _____

12 **Read.** Underline the narrative tenses in the paragraph.

13 **Write.** Reread the prompt from Activity 12. Write your own response using the narrative tenses. Then share your response in a group.

Prompt: Tell about a time when you achieved something important. What did you achieve? How had you been preparing?

Once I climbed a mountain that was over 3,000 m (10,000 ft.) tall. I had been training with my dad all spring to get ready. We had been practicing on smaller mountains. To climb the mountain, we were using special equipment like ice picks and thick ropes. After we had reached the top, it felt great to look down on the forest below us. I later climbed three other mountains with my dad, and we plan to do another next month.

14 **Learn new words.** Listen to the story of Barrington's first solo flight around the world. Then listen and repeat. **TR: 65 and 66**

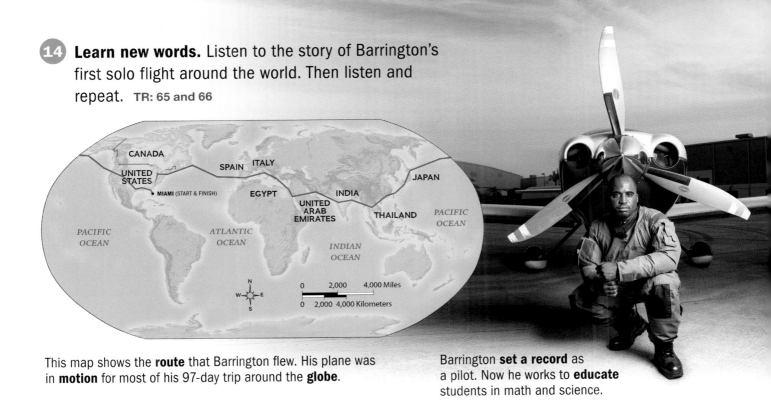

This map shows the **route** that Barrington flew. His plane was in **motion** for most of his 97-day trip around the **globe**.

Barrington **set a record** as a pilot. Now he works to **educate** students in math and science.

15 **Work in pairs.** Read the interview questions and fill in the blanks with the correct words from the box. Then answer the questions as if you were Barrington. Use the narrative tenses.

globe	motion	pilot	route	set a record

1. Q: How had playing video games prepared you to become a _____?

   A: _____

2. Q: How were you able to get an airplane to fly around the _____?

   A: _____

3. Q: How many stops were on your _____?

   A: _____

4. Q: What were you doing to stay awake while in _____ for so many hours?

   A: _____

5. Q: How did you feel when you heard you had _____?

   A: _____

16 **Work independently.** Investigate another person who has explored new places. Write a narrative about the explorer's route, experiences, and accomplishments. Share what you learned with the class.

THE Explorer GENE

Are we born to explore?

Of all the animals on Earth, none are so driven to explore as humans. Other animals will go in search of food or water. But humans can be motivated simply by the possibility of discovery. So what is it exactly that caused us to spread out across the globe 60,000 years ago, instead of just staying in Africa?

Perhaps it's in our DNA. In 1999, Dr. Chuansheng Chen led a team of scientists who were studying a gene known as $DRD_{4-7}R$. This gene is found in about twenty percent of all humans. It's been associated with higher rates of risk-taking, exploration, and interest in new ideas. Dr. Chen found that $DRD_{4-7}R$ is more common in societies that move around a lot than those who don't. For example, studies in Africa show that the gene is much more common in nomadic tribes than in tribes that prefer to stay in one place. Several other researchers have studied this topic and found additional evidence to support Dr. Chen's claim.

Journalist and National Geographic Fellow Paul Salopek is walking from where humans began in Ethiopia, Africa, to the southern tip of South America, following our ancestors' ancient journey.

17 **Before you read, discuss in pairs.** Based on the title and the photo, what do you think you'll learn in this reading?

18 **Learn new words.** Find these words in the reading. What do you think they mean? Look at how they're pronounced in a dictionary. Say them aloud. Then listen and repeat. TR: 67

associated	gene	to motivate	trait

19 While you read, think about a person you know who might have

But can a single gene be responsible for a trait as complex as the desire to explore? Dr. Kenneth Kidd doesn't think so. He thinks $DRD_{4-7}R$ might increase curiosity, but other equally important sets of genes give us intelligent minds and skilled hands. We then use our minds and hands to create things. He believes that not just one gene, but groups of genes work together to create complex behaviors like exploration.

The context we live in also plays a role in our desire to explore. For example, during the European Age of Exploration, explorers became rich and famous for their discoveries. This drove others to try to increase their wealth through exploration. In this case, their exploration was more likely motivated by money than by genes.

Maybe the desire to explore comes from something inside us, such as the $DRD_{4-7}R$ gene. Or maybe it has more to do with what's happening in the world around us. Maybe both. Whatever the reason, it seems we (or at least some of us) will keep exploring the mountains, the sea, the stars, and beyond, because that's just what humans do.

20 **After you read, work in pairs to answer the questions.**

1. What makes humans explore? How are we different from other animals?

2. What traits is the $DRD_{4-7}R$ gene associated with?

3. What percent of humans have this gene?

4. What is Dr. Kenneth Kidd's opinion regarding $DRD_{4-7}R$'s connection to exploration?

5. What else might cause humans

21 **Work in pairs.** Describe the person that you thought of in Activity 19. Give examples to explain why you think this person has the gene.

22 **Discuss in groups.**

1. Do you believe a gene causes humans to explore? Or do you think it has more to do with other factors? Explain.

2. Do you think you have the $DRD_{4-7}R$ gene? Explain, with examples. What other beliefs and behaviors might be caused by something in your genes?

3. Are humans exploring more now than in the

23 **Before you watch, discuss in pairs.** Why is it important to explore?

24 **Watch scene 5.1. While you watch, complete the quotes.**

1. "It's part of _____ to be
   _____ and to want to learn more about the world."

2. "It _____ . I mean that's what exploring
   is about."

3. "We think we know _____ , but we don't. We
   think we know _____ , but we don't. We think
   we _____ , but we don't."

4. "By knowing what's out there, we _____ ."

Explorers camping near the Nyiragongo
volcano, Democratic Republic of the Congo

25 **After you watch, read and circle the correct letter.**

1. Which of the following reasons for exploring is <u>not</u> mentioned in the video?

   a. Exploring helps us engage more fully with our world.
   b. Exploring will make us famous.
   c. Exploring is part of human nature.

2. Why is it important to care about what's out there?

   a. So that we can stop asking questions
   b. So that we can engage with our world and act with love
   c. Because very few people do

3. What do we use to help us explore?

   a. Information about the people who came before us
   b. Information about new species of animals
   c. The high-tech tools of science

4. Why is technology important for exploration?

   a. Because without technology, it's impossible to discover any new animal species.
   b. Because it lets us explore places that are otherwise inaccessible.
   c. Because technology is so important for conservation.

26 **Work in pairs.** Review your answer for Activity 23. Compare it with what you heard in the video. Discuss your comparisons with your partner.

27 **Work in groups.** You're in charge of a school-wide campaign to promote exploration. Create a poster or an advertisement on the benefits of exploring. Present your work to the class.

28 **Choose an activity.**

1. **Work independently.** Research one of the explorers from the video to learn more about his/her work. Share what you learned with the class.

2. **Work in pairs.** Make your own video, similar to this one. Interview other students and ask them, "What can we learn from exploring our region?"

3. **Work in groups.** Research a recent discovery of a new species. Find out who the explorers were, where they went, and what led them to the discovery.

Geographic use of *the*

I'm going to **the Himalayas** to climb **Mt. Everest**.

The Yangtze is the longest river in **Asia**. **Lake Baikal** is the largest lake in **Asia**.

The equator passes through **Isabella Island**, the largest of **the Galápagos Islands**.

Explorer Ferdinand Magellan was born in **Portugal**, but died in **the Philippines**.

Explorer Gertrude Bell wrote a book about **Syria** after her travels to **the Middle East**.

29 **Read.** Fill in the timeline of female explorers by adding *the* when necessary.

1805

Native American Sacagawea guided Lewis and Clark through _____ Oregon Territory of _____ United States.

1908

Mountaineer Annie Smith Peck was the first person to climb _____ Huascarán, a 6,768 m (22,204 ft.) mountain in _____ Peru.

1953

Eugenie Clark wrote a book about studying sharks in _____ South Pacific Ocean and _____ Sea of Cortez, near _____ Mexico.

1894

Mary Kingsley traveled to _____ Sierra Leone, then _____ Gabon and up _____ Ogowe River by canoe, encountering hippos, crocodiles, and gorillas.

1932

Amelia Earhart flew solo across _____ Atlantic Ocean from _____ Canada to _____ Ireland.

30 **Work in pairs.** Cut out the cards and place them face-down. Take turns trying to match the information with the explorer. When you make a match, describe the explorer's work, using the places on the card.

Go to p. 167.

fly solo
Jamaica
Miami
United States

Barrington Irving

WRITING

When we compare and contrast two people, things, or ideas, we use phrases such as the following:

Compare: **in the same way**   **likewise**   **similarly**

Contrast: **by comparison**   **in contrast**   **on one hand . . . on the other hand**

1   **Read the model.** Work in pairs to identify the parts of the writing. How does the writer compare and contrast exploration past and present? Underline the phrases.

Exploration has changed a lot over time. In the past, only adventurers who were willing to take risks were considered explorers. In contrast, anyone can be an explorer today thanks to modern technology.

In the past, when explorers traveled the world, people back home had to wait for months to hear about their adventures. Explorers kept journals and wrote letters about their experiences. They would only be able to tell others what they saw after they returned. By the end of the nineteenth century, explorers were also able to take photos in the same way that they do today. However, they were unable to see the photos right away. It often took a long time for them to get photos printed.

By comparison, today's explorers can travel around the globe and can send back live, real-time images. Thanks to high-tech devices and the Internet, anyone can interact with them. When a discovery is made, we can see photos on social media and read blog posts the same day. We may not be there, but we still take part in the adventure. Similarly, thanks to high-tech cameras and 3D scanners, archeologists and other scientists can now study objects without ever touching or removing them from their sites. This way, people can learn about these things without the risk of harming or breaking them.

There are similarities between exploration in the past and the present. For example, explorers are driven by curiosity and the desire for knowledge about the world. Likewise, people want to share what they discover with others, both in writing and with photos. So, even though the methods may be different, our reasons for exploring have stayed the same over time.

2   **Work in pairs.** How is the way we explore different now compared to the past?

3   **Write.** Write an essay that compares and contrasts exploring out in the field with exploring virtually.

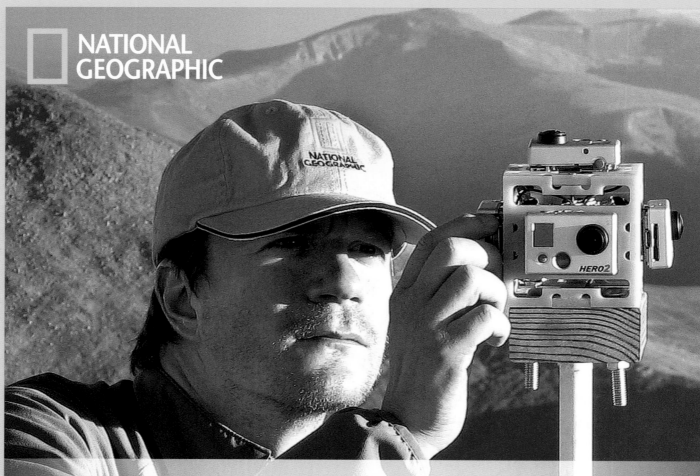

Learn by Doing

"If you have curiosity, you have to be an explorer. You have to go out and find the answers yourself without waiting to get them from others."

—Corey Jaskolski
National Geographic Explorer, Engineer/Inventor

1. **Watch scene 5.2.**

2. How do you learn best—by listening to your teacher or by doing something for yourself? What are the advantages of each type of learning? Talk about a time when you learned something new just by doing it.

3. When you go to a new place, what tools do you use to help you explore? What other tools could you use to learn about another place? Name two or three that you would like to have.

Make an Impact

A **Plan an expedition.**

· Research where you will explore and what you hope to find.

· Plan your expedition. Create an itinerary with photos and a map showing where you plan to explore. Add as much detail as possible.

· Present your plan to the class.

B **Profile a well-known explorer.**

· Research an explorer from the past or present.

· Prepare a biography of the explorer. Include information on where he/she has explored, what he/she has discovered, and his/her methods and tools.

· Create a poster or a computer-based presentation to share what you learned.

C **Explore from home.**

· Research different ways to explore without leaving your home.

· Identify advantages and disadvantages of virtual exploration.

· Write a feature article to describe ways for people to explore virtually. Use examples from your own experience.

Giants

"For as long as humans have been around, they have been fascinated by giant organisms." —Nizar Ibrahim

1. Look at the tree. How old do you think it is? What makes you think this?

2. What's the biggest plant you've ever seen in real life? The biggest animal? Describe them.

3. What do you think of when you hear the word *giant*? Why?

A team of scientists measuring a giant sequoia in Sequoia National Park, California, USA

1 Who were the giants of the past?

Discuss. Then listen and read. TR: 70

Let's go back, deep in time, to the land of the giants, when there were hundreds of species of dinosaurs on Earth. What were they like? And how did they go extinct? Many scientists believe that a major **catastrophe**—a meteor strike—destroyed these **enormous** beasts. Even though they're gone, their fossils can help us to understand what they were like.

Many people think that *Tyrannosaurus rex*, or *T. rex*, is the king of the **ancient** carnivores. It's *T. rex's* size that made this creature so **frightening**—it was **huge**! *T. rex* measured 4.5–6 m (15–20 ft.) tall and 12 m (40 ft.) long. Its eyes were the size of grapefruits, its **stomach** was 1 m (3.3 ft.) in **diameter**, and it used its massive **jaws** to chew up to 230 kg (500 lbs.) of meat in a single bite! *T. rex* had a **heart** the size of a refrigerator, which pumped all the blood through its giant body.

Although *T. rex* was really big, it wasn't the largest **prehistoric** creature ever discovered. That title belongs to *Argentinosaurus*, who measured 40 m (130 ft.) long. This gigantic herbivore's bones were found in Patagonia, Argentina. Babies **weighed** only 5 kg (11 lb.), but adults could weigh up to 75 tons. To reach full size, a young *Argentinosaurus* must have gained up to 5 kilograms per day over 40 years, which made it one of the fastest-growing animals on Earth!

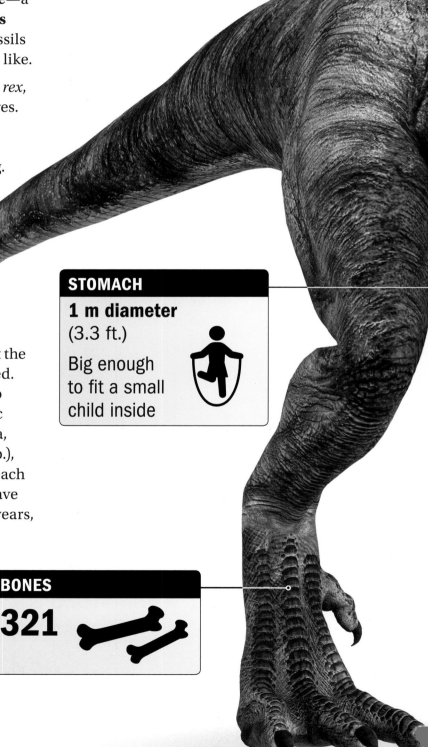

STOMACH

1 m diameter
(3.3 ft.)

Big enough to fit a small child inside

BONES

321

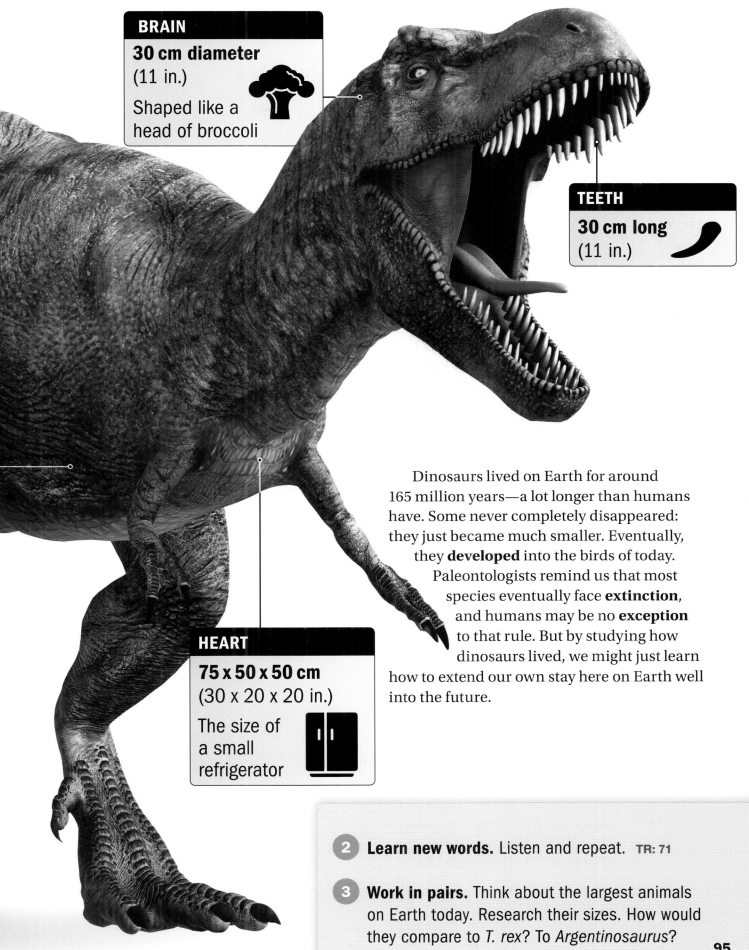

BRAIN

30 cm diameter
(11 in.)

Shaped like a
head of broccoli

TEETH

30 cm long
(11 in.)

HEART

75 x 50 x 50 cm
(30 x 20 x 20 in.)

The size of
a small
refrigerator

Dinosaurs lived on Earth for around
165 million years—a lot longer than humans
have. Some never completely disappeared:
they just became much smaller. Eventually,
they **developed** into the birds of today.
Paleontologists remind us that most
species eventually face **extinction**,
and humans may be no **exception**
to that rule. But by studying how
dinosaurs lived, we might just learn
how to extend our own stay here on Earth well
into the future.

2 **Learn new words.** Listen and repeat. TR: 71

3 **Work in pairs.** Think about the largest animals
on Earth today. Research their sizes. How would
they compare to *T. rex*? To *Argentinosaurus*?

95

4 **Read and write the words from the list.** Make any necessary changes.

ancient	catastrophe	develop	extinction
frightening	huge	jaw	weigh

Nizar Ibrahim has always loved dinosaurs. As a student, he _____ an interest in the work of a famous paleontologist, Dr. Ernst Stromer. One hundred years ago, Dr. Stromer collected bones from the _____ sands of the Sahara Desert. About 100 million years ago, the Sahara Desert was a tropical waterway full of _____ predatory giants. Today Nizar is continuing to learn about what lived in this region. He's most interested in Dr. Stromer's discovery of *Spinosaurus*, a skilled hunter that could catch food in water and on land. *Spinosaurus* was _____ —even bigger than *T. rex*. In fact, *Spinosaurus* had meter-long _____ that it used for catching fish and other aquatic creatures. Dr. Stromer was the first to make significant discoveries about *Spinosaurus*, but Nizar has found more remains of this fascinating giant than anyone else to date.

5 **Learn new words.** Listen for these words. Write *S* next to word pairs that are synonyms and *A* next to antonyms. Then listen and repeat. **TR: 72 and 73**

Nizar Ibrahim

carnivore	gigantic	herbivore	massive

_____ 1. carnivore   herbivore

_____ 2. massive   small

_____ 3. enormous   massive

_____ 4. tiny   gigantic

_____ 5. gigantic   huge

_____ 6. herbivore   plant-eater

6 **Choose an activity.**

1. **Work independently.** Make a poster about a dinosaur you hadn't heard of before. Describe its size, diet, habitat, when it lived, and other characteristics.

2. **Work in pairs.** Research the dinosaurs that once lived in your region. Compare them with wild animals that live in this region today.

3. **Work in groups.** Talk about an encounter with a large animal you've had at a zoo or in the wild.

Speculating about the past and the future

In theory, <u>dinosaurs were destroyed by a global catastrophe</u>.

What may have happened <u>is that they evolved into smaller animals, such as birds</u>.

I wonder <u>how humans will evolve over the next thousand years</u>.

Is it possible that <u>we will become totally different creatures</u>?

It could be that <u>we'll be exactly the same in the year 3000</u>.

7 **Listen.** How do these speakers speculate? Write the phrases you hear. TR: 75

8 **Read and complete the dialogue.**

Nina: _____ which dinosaurs had hair on their bodies.

Rene: You mean fur, like bears and lions have?

Nina: Yeah. You know, we only know what their bones were like so, _____ , some could have had fur or feathers.

Rene: _____ *T. rex* was soft and furry?

Nina: Actually they found a dinosaur similar to *T. rex* in China that was covered in soft feathers—like a baby chick!

Rene: Wow! A massive baby chick? Sounds like a horror movie!

Nina: Well, the ones they found were smaller than *T. rex*, but still about the length of a city bus.

Rene: That's pretty big. _____ why they had feathers?

Nina: _____ is that some dinosaurs grew feathers and fur to stay warm in colder climates.

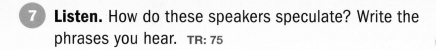

Scientists believe that the large, feathered *Yutyrannus* was 9 m (30 ft.) long and weighed about 1,400 kg (3,000 lb.).

9 **Work in groups.** Cut four strips of paper. Write a question about a prehistoric giant on each of the strips. Mix the group's questions into a single pile. Take turns asking questions and speculating.

I wonder what *T. rex*'s skin was like.

It could be that *T. rex* had very colorful skin.

10 **Work in groups.** Repeat the activity above. This time, choose your own topics to discuss.

Is it possible that our school will offer a class in paleontology?

Relative clauses: Defining and describing

I learned about megalodon in a documentary **that/which** was very informative. It had enormous teeth **that/which** were as sharp as knives.

Scientists **who/that** study sharks believe that megalodon is a distant cousin of the modern great white shark.

The ocean **where/in which** megalodon swam was much warmer than the ocean is today.

Megalodon, **which** was a fierce predator, was able to catch the largest whales.

Scientists such as Catalina Pimiento, **who** researches sharks, have studied reasons for megalodon's extinction.

Megalodon, **whose** name comes from the Greek *giant tooth*, had enormous jaws.

11 **Read.** Complete the sentences below with *that*, *which*, *where*, *who*, or *whose*.

Many people today fear the great white shark, _____ is considered the fiercest predator of the seas. The great white's enormous size is enough to scare off anybody _____ comes near it. This carnivore, _____ measures 4.5–6 m (15–20 ft.), is often believed to prey on humans. In fact, researchers _____ job it is to study shark attacks have determined that the species is responsible for between one-third and one-half of all shark attacks. But the idea _____ the great white seeks out humans who swim in the waters _____ it lives isn't based in reality. Although we're talking about a shark _____ is known for biting, the great white is really just a curious animal. When it sees a human _____ crosses its path, the shark will most likely bite and then release the victim. The fact _____ the great white could bite just because it's curious isn't very comforting. The only good news is that the great white shark, while enormous, is much closer in size to us than its distant cousin, megalodon, a creature _____ was more than double (maybe triple!) its size.

12 **Work in pairs.** Look at Activity 11 again. Cross out any relative clauses that can be removed from the paragraph.

13 **Learn new words.** Listen to the information about megalodon. Then listen and repeat. **TR: 77 and 78**

Megalodon
Ancient Giant of the Sea

Lived 16 million years ago—2 million years ago, during the Miocene **era**

Teeth as long as 18 cm (7 in.)—about 50 **times** the size of a human tooth

Fierce predator that **preyed on** whales and other giant sea creatures

14 **Read and write.** Combine the sentences into one. Use *that*, *which*, *where*, *who*, and *whose*.

1. Megalodon was a fierce predator. It was almost 3 times the size of *T. rex*.

   Megalodon, which was a fierce predator, was almost 3 times the size of T. rex.

2. Megalodon was known for its massive teeth. Its teeth were 18 cm (7 in.) long.

   _____

3. Megalodon had three rows of teeth. Its teeth were as sharp as knives.

   _____

4. Megalodon and whales swam in oceans around the world. Researchers find their remains together in the oceans.

   _____

5. Megalodon lived during the Miocene era. The Miocene era began about 23 million years ago.

   _____

6. Some scientists look for reasons why megalodon went extinct. Their job is to study megalodon.

   _____

15 **Work in groups.** Choose your own topic and write three clues about it on a piece of paper. Use *that*, *which*, *where*, *who*, and *whose* in your sentences. Then read your clue aloud to your group members, who will guess what you're talking about.

> This is the teacher whose job is to teach us about how animals evolve.

> It's our biology teacher, Mr. Johnson.

16 **Before you read, discuss in pairs.** You've been learning about dinosaurs in this unit. Look at the image below. What's different about the dinosaur you'll read about?

17 **Learn new words.** Find the words below in the reading. What do you think they mean? Notice the word parts, and think about what each part means. Then listen and repeat. TR: 79

advantage	extraordinary
significant	useless

18 **While you read, think about how Nizar must have felt about finding *Spinosaurus* remains.** TR: 80

Spinosaurus

Nizar Ibrahim has always been fascinated by dinosaurs. And he's always enjoyed traveling to faraway places. As a paleontologist, he's able to do both. Nizar has spent a lot of time in the Kem Kem, a region in the Sahara Desert along the border of Morocco and Algeria. This region is hot and dry now, but it was once home to a large river where amazing creatures lived: car-sized fish, several different types of crocodile-like creatures, and a large, predatory dinosaur called *Spinosaurus*.

Spinosaurus, which lived in North Africa about 97 million years ago, was an extraordinary creature. It was enormous, with a length of up to 15 m (50 ft.). It had massive jaws like a crocodile, which were an advantage when catching prey. Nizar knew about some of these characteristics from research that had been done on the *Spinosaurus* in the early 1900s by German paleontologist Ernst Stromer. Nizar and his colleagues used Professor Stromer's notes and sketches, the fossils he had found, and CT-scanning technology to piece together a whole *Spinosaurus* skeleton—a digital dinosaur.

What Nizar and his team learned was significant: *Spinosaurus* had dense bones, feet like paddles, and small hind limbs. All of these were characteristic of animals that spent a lot of

DISCOVERING
Spinosaurus

How one determined paleontologist found a river monster in the Sahara time in the water. "We realized that we were dealing with a river monster," said Nizar. "A predatory dinosaur bigger than *T. rex*, the ruler of this ancient river of giants."

Perhaps the only thing more amazing than the creature itself is how Nizar was able to find its skeleton. In 2008, a local man from Erfoud, Morocco, gave Nizar a cardboard box filled with some fossils. A little while later, Italian colleagues contacted Nizar about fossils they received that were extremely similar to the ones he was given. Nizar wanted to find where the fossils came from. If only Nizar could find the man from Erfoud! Nizar didn't even know the man's name. He only had a mental image of a man with a mustache, which wasn't very helpful. Nizar traveled to Morocco anyway, to try to find him. After a long, unsuccessful search, Nizar gave up hope. He was sitting at an outdoor café, drinking tea with a colleague, talking about how it was useless: he would never piece together *Spinosaurus*. Suddenly, he looked up and saw the man walking down the street. He had found the missing link! The fossil hunter took Nizar to the site, and he was finally able to locate the remaining bones for his *Spinosaurus* skeleton.

19 **After you read, work in pairs to decide if each sentence is *true* or *false*.** Check the correct answer.

1. The Kem Kem region has a large river running through it. Ⓣ Ⓕ

2. Nizar was the first scientist to discover *Spinosaurus*. Ⓣ Ⓕ

3. *Spinosaurus* was larger than *T. rex*. Ⓣ Ⓕ

4. The only thing that really helped Nizar understand *Spinosaurus* was the CT-scanning technology. Ⓣ Ⓕ

5. Dense bones, feet like paddles, and small hind limbs are characteristics of animals that spend time in the water. Ⓣ Ⓕ

6. The man in Morocco gave Nizar all of *Spinosaurus's* bones in a cardboard box. Ⓣ Ⓕ

20 **Work independently.** Imagine you're Nizar. Write a journal entry about finding the *Spinosaurus* bones. How does the discovery make you feel? Why?

21 **Discuss in groups.**

1. What are the advantages of studying dinosaurs? What are the challenges facing paleontologists? Is it worth it to study dinosaurs? Why or why not?

2. What personality traits does Nizar have that helped him to find *Spinosaurus*? Do you have any of these traits? How do you use them?

3. Nizar uses new technology, combined with fossils and old documents, to understand *Spinosaurus*. Name another way that new technology can be used to help people understand something very old.

Nizar and his team looking for fossils in the Sahara

22 **Before you watch, discuss in pairs.**

1. Look again at the photo on pp. 92–93. Comment on the size of the tree in comparison with the people.

2. Look at the timeline on this page. Note the dates when it begins and ends. What do you think they represent?

23 **Work in pairs.** The title of this video is *Super Tree.* You'll see a team of photographers and scientists photographing one of the largest trees in the world, in winter. Predict three challenges that they face.

24 Watch scene 6.1. **While you watch, check your predictions from Activity 23.** Were they correct? Did the team face any other challenges? What were they?

25 **After you watch, work in pairs.** Answer the questions below.

1. What makes the President unique?

2. Describe the President in relation to yourself.

3. How long did it take the team to prepare for the photo shoot? Why do you think that is?

4. Why did these scientists go through so much effort to photograph a tree?

5. The team thinks that the President may be the biggest tree because it has the most biomass. What do you think the word *biomass* means?

2012
Scientists climb the President, the second-largest living tree.

1969
The first person lands on the moon.

1707
Mount Fuji erupts in Japan.

1325
The Aztecs establish the city of Tenochtitlan.

868 CE
The earliest known book is printed.

221 BCE
Construction of the Great Wall of China begins.

1100 BCE
Nearly 100 years after this tree sprouts, people begin making iron tools.

---

26 **Work in pairs.** Read and cross out the false sentences. Then rewrite them correctly.

1. There is only one species of California redwoods.

   _____

2. The bigger the tree, the less it's producing.

   _____

3. The President has been growing for over 3,000 years.

   _____

4. At over 8 m (27 ft.) in diameter, the President has the largest trunk of any tree.

   _____

   _____

5. The horrible snowstorm is making the team members want to cry.

   _____

   _____

27 **Work in groups.** Look at the timeline. Think of five more significant events that have happened during this tree's lifetime. List them in the order they occur.

28 **Choose an activity.**

1. **Work independently.** Photograph something very large in your community. Be sure to get the entire object into your photograph. Display your photo(s) in class and talk about the process of capturing the object.

2. **Work in pairs.** In the video, scientists work together to photograph a big tree. Think of another situation you've heard or read about where people came together to work with a big animal or plant. Why are so many people needed to work with giant things?

3. **Work in groups.** Find out about another well-known big tree. Say where it is, how big it is, and how old it is. Share a photo and describe it.

Reduction of relative clauses

My brother, **(who is) a filmmaker**, created a documentary about manta rays.

The documentaries **(that) I was telling you about** deal with sea creatures.

One of the documentaries is about a new species **(that/which was) discovered** last year.

The scientists **(that/who) I saw** in the documentaries were really interesting.

The biologist **that/who studies** manta rays lives in Mozambique. (The biologist **studying** manta rays . . .)

29 **Read.** Cross out unnecessary words to reduce the clauses.

You read about the giants of the past. But there are plenty of giants still alive today who are living in the sea. The blue whale, which is the largest animal of all time, is still with us today. Many other giants live underwater as well. Andrea Marshall, who is a conservation biologist, studies these *marine megafauna*, or giant, underwater animals. Much of her work focuses on the enormous manta rays that are living off the coast of Mozambique. Manta rays are

A manta ray

threatened because they're being harmed by human activity and they don't reproduce often. In 2009, Andrea founded the Marine Megafauna Foundation, which is an organization that works to protect large marine animals such as the manta ray. One of her proudest moments came in 2013, which was the year she got special protection for the manta ray. "Mantas are some of the most engaging and charismatic underwater animals you'll ever encounter," says Andrea. "They're so curious and smart, always ready to interact and play with you."

30 **Read.** Rewrite the sentences, reducing the clauses.

1. Biologist Andrea Marshall, who is known for protecting marine megafauna, focuses on the manta ray.

   Biologist Andrea Marshall, known for protecting marine megafauna, focuses on the manta ray.

2. The manta rays that Marshall studies don't reproduce very often.

   _____

3. The manta rays that swim in the waters off Mozambique are in need of protection.

   _____

31 **Work in groups.** Cut out the cards. Take turns reading the sentences aloud and reducing the clauses.

Go to p. 169.

The *T-rex*, which was the fiercest land predator of its time, had huge jaws and teeth.

WRITING

When writing a news report, we should consider the five *W*s: *who*, *what*, *where*, *when*, and *why*, as well as *how*. Answering these questions early on can capture the reader's interest, and make him/her want to learn more. Answering these questions will also provide all the necessary details about the situation in the report.

32 **Read the model.** Work in pairs. Identify the five *W*s and *how* in the news report.

Capturing a Giant: Enormous Tree Photographed in Sequoia National Park

Sequoia National Park, California, is the land of the giants. The giants are the sequoias, the largest species of trees on the planet. A few among them are so extraordinary they have names. The President is one of the largest trees in the world. It was recently studied by scientist Steve Sillett. In 2012, Sillett and his team photographed the entire 75 m (246 ft.) tree. Because the tree was too large to get in one photo, Sillett's team of photographers combined several photos of the tree into one complete shot. This project was done to educate people about these enormous trees, and all of the life they support.

One of the most interesting discoveries Sillett's team made is that sequoias never stop growing. As the tree continues to grow, it competes with other plants for soil, light, and water. The President has been growing for 3,200 years. Because of their size, sequoias can defend themselves well against threats like wind and fire. Even lightning strikes usually fail to harm them.

The National Park Service estimates that over 260 forest plants, animals, and insects depend on the sequoias, and over 150 of those life forms are rare or uncommon. Humans also depend on the sequoias to break down huge amounts of carbon dioxide, providing cleaner air for breathing.

Sillett hopes his work will not only inspire the public to help protect these giants, but also encourage more tall-tree research throughout the world.

33 **Work in pairs.** Look at the structure of the report. Where does the author answer the five *W*s? How? Does the report make you want to learn more about the topic? Why or why not?

34 **Write.** Write a news report about a giant discovery of the past or present. Use a topic from this unit or another giant discovery that interests you.

Make Big Plans

"The world is not made for us, and we are privileged to be here and should make the most of it."

—Nizar Ibrahim

National Geographic Explorer, Paleontologist

1. **Watch scene 6.2.**

2. Nizar Ibrahim has made big plans during his career as a paleontologist. He has already accomplished some of them. What are your big plans? When will you accomplish them?

3. Why do you think Nizar says that we're privileged to be here? Do you feel this way? Why or why not?

Make an Impact

(A) **Make an animated action movie.**

· Write a script for an action movie starring one
of the giants in this unit. Draw the main
scenes on separate pieces of paper.

· Place the scenes in front of a video camera.
Press record and narrate the scene. Then pause, place
the next scene in front of the camera, and repeat.

· After all the scenes have been shot, share your movie with
the class.

(B) **Create and play a "Find the Fossil" game.**

· Find six different images of fossils of the giants you learned
about in this unit. Find six images of the creature to which each
fossil corresponds.

· Create a memory game. Paste the fossil images on one set of
cards. Paste the creatures on another set of cards.

· Place the cards face-down. In pairs, take turns looking for
matches. When you find a match, name the creature and one
of its features. The person with the most cards wins.

(C) **Plan and give a presentation on a modern giant.**

· Research the largest animals on the planet today. Choose
one and learn about its size, appearance, habitat, and diet.

· Create a poster or computer presentation on your animal.
Include photos and statistics to illustrate its size. Compare
the animal with the prehistoric giants studied in this unit.

· Make your presentation in class. Answer your classmates'
questions.

Express Yourself

1 **Read and listen to the adaptation of an excerpt from *A Journey to the Center of the Earth.*** TR: 82

Tuesday, August 18

Evening came, or rather the time came when sleep weighs down the tired eyes, for there is no night here. Hans was controlling the raft. During his watch, I slept.

Two hours later a terrible shock awoke me. The raft was lifted up on a very high wave, and then dropped again.

"What is the matter? Axel? Hans?" shouted my uncle, Professor Otto Lidenbrock. "Have we struck land?"

Hans pointed with his finger at a dark mass over five hundred meters away, rising and falling in the water. I looked and cried, "It is an enormous porpoise."

"Yes," replied my uncle, "and there is a sea lizard of massive size."

"And farther on a monstrous crocodile. Look at its giant jaws and its rows of teeth! It is diving down!"

"There's a whale, a whale!" cried the professor.

We stood amazed, at the presence of such a herd of marine monsters. They were of enormous size; the smallest of them would have crunched our raft, crew and all, at one snap of its huge jaws.

Getting away was out of the question now. The reptiles rose; they circled around our little raft faster than express trains.

We stood dumb with fear. At nearly three hundred meters from us the battle was fought. We could see the two monsters engaged in deadly conflict. But it now seems to me as if the other animals were taking part, too—the porpoise, the whale, the lizard, the tortoise. Every moment I seem to see one or the other of them. I point them to Hans. He shakes his head negatively.

"*Tva*," he says.

"What *two*? Does he mean that there are only two animals?"

"He is right," said my uncle.

"Surely you must be mistaken," I cried.

"No: the first of those monsters has a porpoise's snout, a lizard's head, a crocodile's teeth. It is the *ichthyosaurus* (the fish lizard), the most terrible of the ancient monsters of the deep."

"And the other?"

"The other is a *plesiosaurus* (almost lizard), a serpent, with the characteristics of a turtle. He is the enemy of the other."

Hans had spoken truly. Two monsters only were creating all this commotion, and before my eyes are two reptiles of the ancient world. I can distinguish the eye of the *ichthyosaurus* glowing like a red-hot coal, and as large as a man's head. This one is not less than thirty meters long, and I can judge of its size when it shows its tail. Its jaw is enormous, and according to naturalists it is armed with no less than one hundred and eighty-two teeth.

The *plesiosaurus*, a serpent with a tube-shaped body and a short tail, has four flappers or paddles. Its body is entirely covered with scales, and its neck, as flexible as a swan's, rises nine meters above the waves.

Those huge creatures attacked each other with the greatest hatred.

2 **Discuss in groups.**

1. The characters are exploring the center of the Earth. How do you imagine the center of the Earth looks? How do the picture and the text compare with your own ideas?

2. Imagine you're on this journey. Describe how you feel when you see the ancient creatures fighting in the sea.

3. Describe the *ichthyosaurus* and the *plesiosaurus* in your own words. Compare them with the giant creatures you studied in Unit 6.

3 **Connect ideas.** In Unit 5, you learned about exploration and discovery. In Unit 6, you learned about giants past and present. How does the reading passage connect these two units? Do you think that real-life explorers ever had experiences similar to those of Axel, Hans, and Professor Lidenbrock? Explain.

4 **Choose an activity.**

1. Choose a topic:
   - exploration
   - giant discoveries

2. Choose a way to express yourself:
   - the next scene of the story
   - an action/adventure skit
   - a podcast describing an adventure or a discovery

3. Present your work.

Creative Problem-Solving

A creative way to bring the
dog along, Taipei

"People create amazing things based on what they can imagine, and what they're truly, truly passionate and excited about."
—Tan Le

1. What problem is the man in the photo solving? Can you think of another way to solve the problem?

2. Think of an invention that impressed you. Who made it? How is it useful? Why is it interesting to you?

3. How does an idea become a reality? What needs to happen in order to successfully create something?

111

Have you ever had a problem you couldn't **solve**? Maybe you went to the store to look for a solution, but came home empty-handed. More and more, when this situation occurs, people are creating their own **devices** as the solution. It's all part of the Maker Movement, made up of thousands of **resourceful** people who make and fix things, rather than buy them in stores. Makers do all sorts of **hands-on** projects, from building pizza ovens to designing their own drones. For makers, the **do-it-yourself** approach is often more affordable, sustainable, and satisfying than simply looking to buy the solution to a problem.

Thanks to technology, it's easier than ever to turn a **concept** into reality. Many makers use the same tools, just in different ways. For example, Arduino® is popular among makers. This **open-source** mini controller is used to develop a variety of electronic devices. Arduino allows people to do anything from creating a talking clock to studying DNA, with very easy-to-use **hardware** and **software**. Raspberry Pi® is another popular maker tool. This mini computer is only the size of a credit card, but it's as powerful as some full-sized computers. People are using Raspberry Pi for a wide variety of **applications**, from creating video games to powering robots.

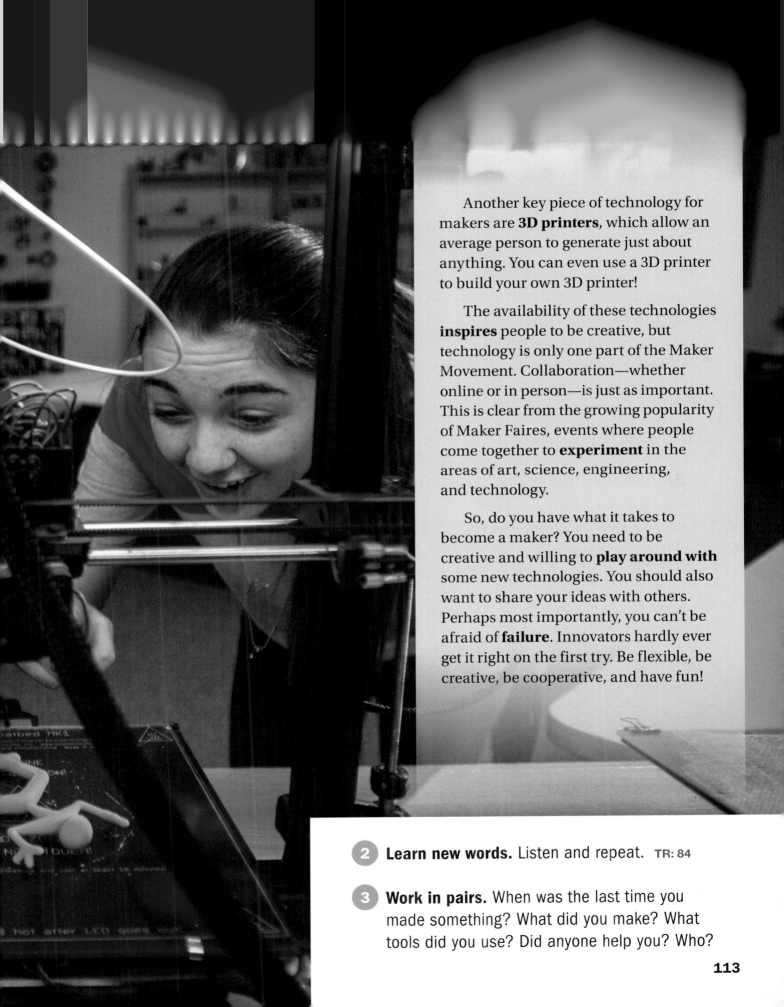

Another key piece of technology for makers are **3D printers**, which allow an average person to generate just about anything. You can even use a 3D printer to build your own 3D printer!

The availability of these technologies **inspires** people to be creative, but technology is only one part of the Maker Movement. Collaboration—whether online or in person—is just as important. This is clear from the growing popularity of Maker Faires, events where people come together to **experiment** in the areas of art, science, engineering, and technology.

So, do you have what it takes to become a maker? You need to be creative and willing to **play around with** some new technologies. You should also want to share your ideas with others. Perhaps most importantly, you can't be afraid of **failure**. Innovators hardly ever get it right on the first try. Be flexible, be creative, be cooperative, and have fun!

2 **Learn new words.** Listen and repeat. TR: 84

3 **Work in pairs.** When was the last time you made something? What did you make? What tools did you use? Did anyone help you? Who?

113

4 **Read and write the words from the list.** Make any necessary changes.

3D printer	application	concept	device	failure
hands-on	inspire	play around with	software	solve

When entrepreneur Tan Le was a kid, she wanted to move objects with her mind. Now she creates headsets that allow people to do just that. The headsets scan our brains and enable us to _____ problems just by thinking about them! Tan's original _____ was to create a _____ that was lightweight and easy to use. She and her team _____ many different models. Although they encountered problems, it never stopped them from working toward their goal. Tan saw both _____ and success as equal parts of the process. Eventually, she and her team created the first wearable brain scanner using EEG, the Emotiv Insight. The headset has a lot of _____ , especially helping people do things with their minds instead of their bodies. The scanner is also important in helping researchers understand how a healthy human brain works.

5 **Learn new words.** Listen for these words and match them to their definitions. Then listen and repeat.

TR: 85 and 86

Tan Le uses her mind to control the robot on the screen.

affordable	approach	flexible	innovator

_____ 1. not expensive

_____ 2. willing to change or try different things

_____ 3. a person who introduces new ideas

_____ 4. a way of doing something

6 **Choose an activity.**

1. **Work independently.** Use the Internet to learn more about do-it-yourself projects. Make a list of five that interest you. Present your favorite project to the class.

2. **Work in pairs.** Survey at least five other students to determine if they are makers. If they are, what do they make? Why? If they aren't, why not? What would they be interested in making? Report your findings to the class.

3. **Work in groups.** Think of a device or app that could solve a problem you have. Does it exist? If so, describe how it works. If not, explain what could be created and how it would help you.

Asking someone to defend an opinion

Why do you think <u>it's important to make things yourself</u>?

Are you sure <u>it's cheaper to make it than to buy it</u>?

What makes you think that?

Can you explain <u>why you think we need to create a device</u>?

So you think <u>the Maker Movement is helping people be more creative</u>?

A 3D printer

7 Listen. How does David's mom ask him to defend his opinions? Write the phrases you hear. TR: 88

8 Read and complete the dialogue.

Liz: Dad, look at my cookie cutter designs. I'm going to print them with the school's 3D printer and then sell them online.

Dad: _____ that will be OK with your school?

Liz: Yeah, I'm sure. Actually it started as a school project, but I think I could really make some money selling them.

Dad: _____ people will buy them?

Liz: Well, my teacher really liked my designs. And my friends have already bought some.

Dad: _____ how you'll do this exactly?

Liz: People could buy the cookie cutters I have designed and made. Or they could design their own cookie cutters, and I could print them for them.

Dad: _____ the school will be OK with you using *their* 3D printer for *your* business? _____

Liz: Because it's a learning experience for me—and I'll give the school half the profits!

9 Work in groups. On separate strips of paper, write three sentences that give an opinion on technology use. Combine the group's papers into a pile. Take turns reading an opinion and asking the group member who wrote it to defend it.

> Right now, people spend too much time using smartphones.

> What makes you think that?

10 Work in pairs. Think of a problem you have and brainstorm ways that technology can solve it. Discuss your ideas with a partner. Ask your partner to defend his/her opinions when possible.

Wish and *if only*: Expressing wishes and regrets

I wish I were at the technology fair right now.

I wish my teacher had told me about the fair before today.

I wish the invitations would go directly to students.

If only we were at the technology fair! We could see a demonstration of the EEG headset.

If only Tan had been invited to our school! She could have shown us her invention here.

11 Listen. Listen as the speaker introduces Tan and her Emotiv Insight headset at a technology fair. Select the most logical reaction from each pair, based on what you heard. TR: 90

1. **a.** I wish I knew what Tan did.
   b. I wish I could experiment with Tan's headset.

2. **a.** I can't believe the technology is open-source. If only I knew how to use it correctly.
   b. If only the technology were open-source! Then, anyone could access it.

3. **a.** I wish Tan would develop ways for disabled people to use the headset.
   b. If only every disabled person had one of these headsets!

4. **a.** If only drivers had used the headset to communicate with each other. Then, the accident wouldn't have happened.
   b. If only drivers had used the headset to help them pay attention. Then, the accident wouldn't have happened.

5. **a.** I wish I were part of the experiment to have my thoughts 3D printed!
   b. I wish I were a child so that I could get a toy headset.

12 Work independently. Listen to the audio again. Imagine that you had an EEG headset for a day. Write sentences expressing wishes and regrets about the experience. TR: 91

1. *If only I had been given an EEG headset to keep! I would have shown it to everyone.*

2. _____

   _____

3. _____

   _____

13 Work in pairs. Rewrite the sentences below to express wishes and regrets.

1. I never learned to program computers. _If only I had learned to program computers._

_____

2. My brother doesn't let me use his computer. _____

_____

3. You broke my smartphone. Now we can't play video games! _____

_____

4. My school didn't buy a 3D printer this year. _____

_____

14 Learn new words. Listen to information about an interesting use for EEG headsets. Then listen and repeat. **TR: 92 and 93**

British musician Daniel Stein, widely known as DJ Fresh, organized the *Mindtunes* project. In it, he helped **disabled** musicians **transform** their thoughts into music. **Wireless** EEG headsets **interpret** signals from their brains. They link these signals to electronic sounds, which the musicians can "play" with their minds.

15 Work in pairs. Write sentences about wishes or regrets using the words provided.

1. interpret my thoughts _____

_____

2. transform into reality _____

_____

3. use a wireless device _____

_____

4. help disabled people _____

_____

16 Work in groups. Write two things that you wish you had or could do. Write two things that you wish you had done. Discuss your wishes and regrets with your group.

17 Before you read, discuss in pairs. Based on the title and the photos, what do you think you'll learn in this reading?

18 Learn new words. Find these words in the reading. Use a dictionary to find their meanings. Think of antonyms you know for any of the words. Then listen and repeat. TR: 94

to amount to	to discourage	persistent
success	to turn away	

19 While you read, take notes on the failures and successes of the people described. TR: 95

20 After you read, work in pairs to answer the questions.

1. What did J.K. Rowling think of herself before she became famous?
2. Describe the success of the *Harry Potter* series.
3. What did Albert Einstein's teachers think of him?
4. Why couldn't Einstein find a job after graduation?
5. What was the first electronic device that Masaru Ibuka and Akio Morita made? What was the outcome?
6. What product made their company successful?

21 Work in pairs. Using your notes, create a chart to categorize the failures and successes of each person described in the text.

GREAT

You've learned about Tan Le's incredible innovation, but that didn't come instantly. Tan and her team tried many times before finding success. And Tan's not alone. In fact, for many, success is the result of overcoming great failure.

J.K. Rowling's *Harry Potter* books have sold more than 450 million copies, and have been translated into 77 languages. But before she became famous, Rowling said of herself, "I was as poor as it is possible to be . . . I was the biggest failure I knew." She sent her first book to 12 publishers, but they all rejected it. However, Rowling was persistent. After a year of trying, a publisher finally accepted her manuscript. *Harry Potter and the Philosopher's Stone* became the first novel in a series that would become the best-selling young adult books of all time.

J.K. Rowling

FAILURES

PEOPLE WHO LEARNED TO TRY AND TRY AGAIN

Albert Einstein

When you hear the name Albert Einstein, you probably think *genius*. But many of Einstein's teachers thought he was lazy and wouldn't amount to anything. When he applied to university, he was turned away because he failed the exams. He spent an entire year preparing to retake them before he was accepted. After graduation, he struggled to get a job because none of his teachers was willing to give him a recommendation. However, Einstein was determined and worked hard. While he worked as a clerk, he continued his studies. He eventually published papers with his theories, and these works changed the field of science. In 1921, Einstein was awarded the Nobel Prize for physics.

Japanese businessmen Masaru Ibuka and Akio Morita met during World War II. After the war, they started a company repairing radios. When they visited a house to repair a radio, they would receive a bag of rice in addition to payment for their work. This gave them the idea to build and sell rice cookers. Unfortunately, their rice cookers didn't work very well, always over- or under-cooking the rice. But this failure didn't discourage Ibuka and Morita. They continued experimenting with electronics. Their company, Sony®, found success making portable radios. The Walkman® made Sony one of the most successful companies in the world. Today, Sony is known for everything from electronics to movies.

These stories show us that failure isn't a sign of losing. In fact, it's part of the process. As Tan says, "It's like two sides to a coin—you can't have success without failure."

Akio Morita and Masaru Ibuka

22 Discuss in groups.

1. What role did failure play in the success of J.K. Rowling, Albert Einstein, Masaru Ibuka, and Akio Morita? What other factors do you think contributed to their successes?

2. How do you deal with failure? Describe a failure you have overcome.

23 **Before you watch, discuss in groups.**

1. In some parts of the world, children, especially girls, are unable to go to school. Why do you think this is?
2. How would your life be different if you weren't able to go to school?

24 **Work in pairs.** The title of this video is *Sanga's Solution*. It's about energy innovator and National Geographic Explorer Sanga Moses. What do you think it means to be an "energy innovator"? Predict why Sanga would feel the need to become an energy innovator.

25 Watch scene 7.1. **While you watch, check your prediction from Activity 24.**

Sanga Moses

26 **After you watch, read the sentences below.** Use the information from the video to decide if each one is *true* or *false*. Check the correct letter.

1. Sanga had a good job in the city. (T) (F)
2. Sanga's sister was crying because she couldn't go to school. (T) (F)
3. Sanga decided to bring his sister into the city so that she could have a better life. (T) (F)
4. Sanga couldn't quit his job, so he worked on the problem from the city. (T) (F)
5. Sanga was able to solve the problem on his own. (T) (F)
6. Sanga's new company uses waste from agricultural products to create clean fuel. (T) (F)

27 **Work in pairs.** Answer the questions below.

1. What does Sanga's company produce and sell?
2. Who does this product help? How?

28 **Work in groups.** Imagine that you have been asked to sell Sanga's product. Create a commercial that advertises at least three benefits to using the product. Share your commercial with the class.

29 **Choose an activity.**

1. **Work independently.** Sanga's idea is an example of "frugal innovation," or creating something new with very little money or resources. Research other examples of people doing more with less. Share some examples with the class.

2. **Work in pairs.** Compare and contrast Sanga Moses and Tan Le. As innovators, how are they similar? How are they different?

3. **Work in groups.** Do some students regularly miss school in your region? Why is this a problem? What might be a solution? Explain your ideas to the class.

Adverbs: Expressing different levels of intensity

Inventor Kelvin Doe is **so** clever.

But he is **rather** shy.

His inventions work **really** well.

Things changed **kind of** quickly for him.

Kelvin **certainly** knows how to be innovative.

Kelvin can **hardly** wait to share his next invention.

30 **Listen.** Learn about teen inventors. Circle the word that best completes the sentences, based on what you hear. TR: 97

1. Kelvin *certainly / sort of* learned a lot in the United States, but he *hardly / really* wanted to return to his community in Sierra Leone.

2. Deepika Kurup realized that for some people, there was *absolutely / barely* enough clean water to live on, so she created an invention to change that.

3. Kenneth Shinozuka's smart socks have been *kind of / very* important for Alzheimer's patients and their caregivers.

4. People who suffer from Alzheimer's can *hardly / really* do anything without a caregiver present.

5. While caring for his family's cows, Richard Turere discovered that the lions that threatened the cows reacted *quite / slightly* negatively to bright, flashing lights.

Deepika Kurup

31 **Work in pairs.** Listen to the information again. Using the words provided, write two additional sentences about the teen inventors. TR: 98

1. extremely _____

2. sort of _____

32 **Work in groups.** Cut out the cards and place them in two piles. Choose a card from each pile. Comment on the topic you get using the word on the other card.

It must have been kind of scary for Kenneth to see his grandfather wandering off.

Go to p. 171.

kind of

Kenneth Shinozuka
created sensors to help his grandfather and other Alzheimer's patients.

WRITING

When you write an exemplification essay, you present a topic and then use examples to explain it. Well-chosen examples can support your writing by making it more accurate, believable, and interesting. Use the following to introduce your examples:

for instance	**a good example is**	**to illustrate**
in particular	**specifically**	**such as**

33 **Read the model.** Work in pairs to identify the parts of the writing. How does the writer signal examples? Underline the phrases.

The other day, while I was at the library, I lost a button on my favorite shirt. I was so upset! It was covered in fabric to match the shirt, so I couldn't replace it. After a few moments of helping me search for the lost button, the librarian asked me if I had clear nail polish. I said I had some at home, so she gave me a tip—cover the buttons on a shirt with clear nail polish and they will stay on better. So I tried it on a different shirt, and it worked!

After learning this trick, I went online to see if there were any other uses for clear nail polish. It turns out there are many. A good example is that clear nail polish can help you thread a needle. Just put a little on the thread, and it will go right through the eye of a needle.

Of course, clear nail polish is useful for things other than sewing! In particular, it can be used to keep things clean and shiny. For instance, if you paint the bottoms of metal containers with clear nail polish, they won't leave rust stains on your shelf. Put some on your belt buckle or costume jewelry, and it will stay shiny forever. Painting jewelry will also decrease the chance that the jewelry will harm your skin.

You can also use clear nail polish to keep things in place, such as screws. Paint the screw before putting it into the wall, and it will stay in better. Cover a broken piece of wood with clear nail polish, and you won't get splinters. Some people even use clear nail polish to relieve the itch of insect bites!

I don't think I'll use clear nail polish on my nails anymore. It has too many other practical uses!

34 **Work in pairs.** What are the problems that the writer can solve using clear nail polish? Make a list.

35 **Write.** Write an exemplification essay. Name a common problem and describe how an everyday object could be used to solve it.

Don't Give Up

"Part of the process is figuring out what doesn't work as much as what does work."

—Tan Le

National Geographic Explorer, Innovator and Entrepreneur

1. Watch scene 7.2.

2. Tan likes to collaborate with others in her work. Do you think it's important to work with others when doing or making new things? How can being part of a team prevent you from quitting or giving up on something?

3. Think of a time when you gave up on something. Why did you give up? What would have happened if you hadn't?

Make an Impact

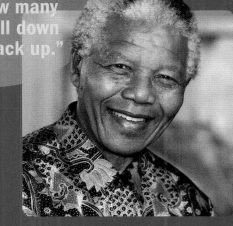

Nelson Mandela

A Pitch an idea.

- Think of a new idea to solve a problem.
- Create a model or a visual to help explain your idea.
- Pitch your idea to the class. Judges choose the best one.

B Profile a successful person who has experienced failure.

- Research successful people who have experienced great failures. Choose one to write about.
- Find out about the person's life. Take notes on his/her failures as well as successes.
- Create a profile of this person. Include photos. Present your profile to the class.

"When you lose, you get up, you make it better, you try again."

Serena Williams

C Design and advertise your own app.

- Think of a new application for an electronic device.
- Design an example of your app by drawing or creating one or two sample screens. Describe how it will work.
- Create a short advertisement for your app that would appear online in an app store.

"If I try my best and fail, well, I've tried my best."

Steve Jobs

Boys looking at art from the *Streets of Afghanistan* exhibit, Afghanistan

Art Connections

"At our core, people are visual communicators."
—Stephen Alvarez

1. What are the people in the photo looking at? What might they be thinking?

2. Who do you communicate with visually? How do you do it?

3. French artist Edgar Degas said, "Art is not what you see, but what you make others see." What do you think he means by this? Do you agree with him? Why or why not?

127

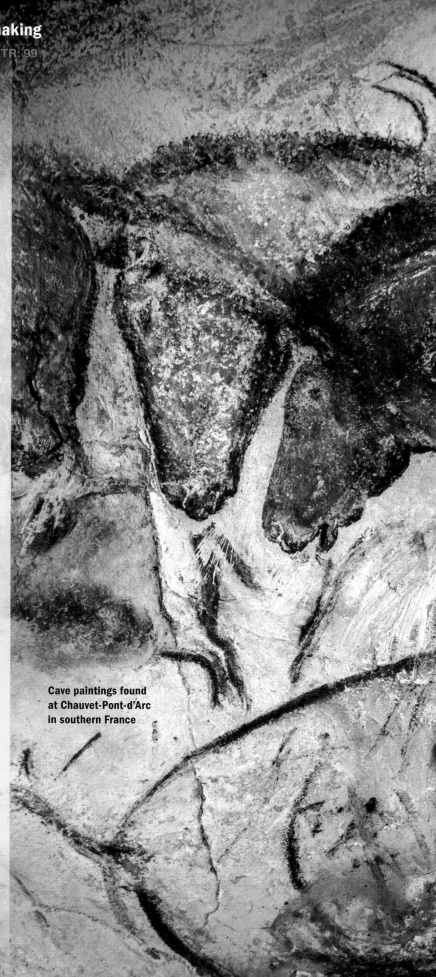

Art is part of the human experience. People have **come up with** many reasons to create **artwork**—some simple, and others more complex. Art can be purely decorative, or it might be created to generate a certain **reaction**. Art also allows an artist to leave a permanent **mark** on time. A painting or sculpture allows the artist to **preserve** a moment that has long passed.

When did art begin? Well, that's a very **controversial** question. Researchers have been working for decades to **track down** the answer. Some have found triangular drawings on rocks in South Africa that are 75,000 years old. They believe that these triangles are art because they're symbolic of something, though there's no way to know for sure what they represent. Other experts don't think that this finding is that impressive. They argue that the images on the rocks don't **depict** any meaningful message. They suggest that we look to walls, specifically cave walls, to find the origins of art.

Sophisticated paintings from nearly 40,000 years ago have been found in caves in Europe and Asia. A red circle on a wall inside the El Castillo cave in Spain is the oldest known cave art at 40,800 years old. When cave art was first studied in Spain in 1880, researchers felt that it was the **accomplishment** of the earliest humans who migrated from Africa to Europe.

Cave paintings found at Chauvet-Pont-d'Arc in southern France

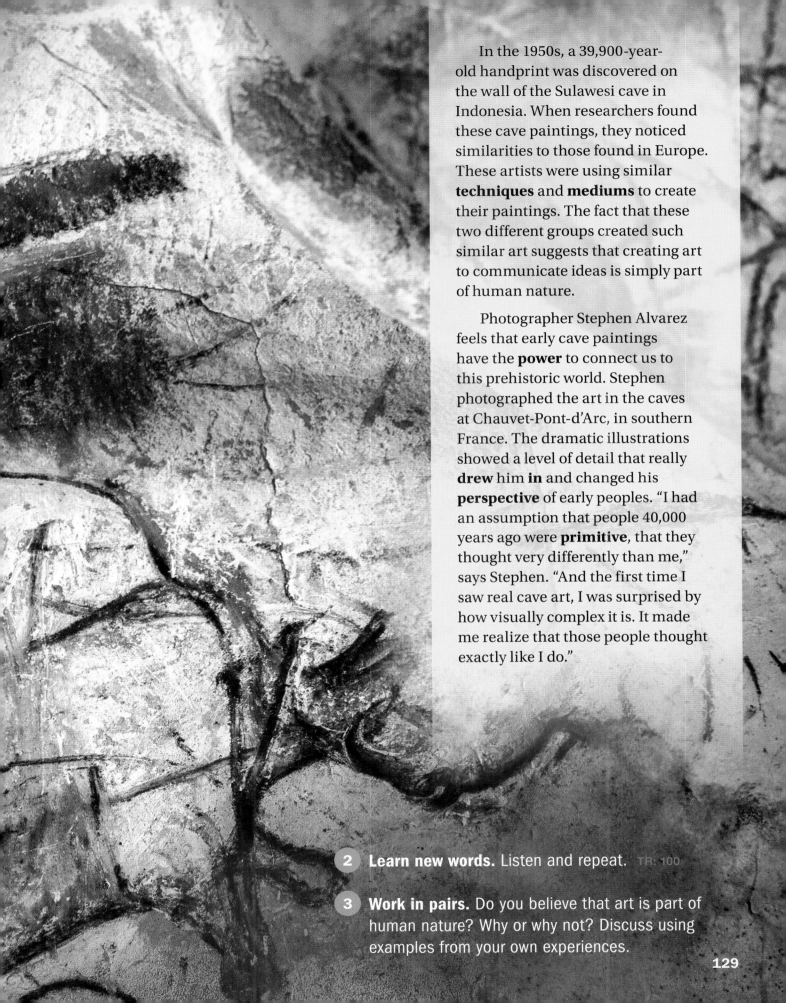

In the 1950s, a 39,900-year-old handprint was discovered on the wall of the Sulawesi cave in Indonesia. When researchers found these cave paintings, they noticed similarities to those found in Europe. These artists were using similar **techniques** and **mediums** to create their paintings. The fact that these two different groups created such similar art suggests that creating art to communicate ideas is simply part of human nature.

Photographer Stephen Alvarez feels that early cave paintings have the **power** to connect us to this prehistoric world. Stephen photographed the art in the caves at Chauvet-Pont-d'Arc, in southern France. The dramatic illustrations showed a level of detail that really **drew** him **in** and changed his **perspective** of early peoples. "I had an assumption that people 40,000 years ago were **primitive**, that they thought very differently than me," says Stephen. "And the first time I saw real cave art, I was surprised by how visually complex it is. It made me realize that those people thought exactly like I do."

2 **Learn new words.** Listen and repeat. TR: 100

3 **Work in pairs.** Do you believe that art is part of human nature? Why or why not? Discuss using examples from your own experiences.

129

4 **Read and write the words from the list.** Make any necessary changes.

accomplishment	artwork	come up with	draw in	medium
power	preserve	reaction	technique	track down

Photography is Stephen Alvarez's preferred _____ for sharing with the rest of us what's hidden underground. As a National Geographic photographer, Stephen travels around the world, and into it, to _____ the best, most powerful images of caves. He has to _____ effective _____ , such as providing extra lighting, to deal with the challenges of taking photos in such dark areas.

Stephen was really impressed by the _____ on the walls in the Chauvet-Pont-d'Arc cave in France when he photographed it in 2014. He had an incredible _____ to photographing this cave art: a feeling of connection to the artists from 36,000 years ago. "I wanted to photograph the paintings in a way that let the original artist's voice come through while also _____ the sense of what it is like to stand in front of that art." Stephen was amazed by the _____ of the art to connect him with these early peoples.

5 **Learn new words.** Listen for these words and match them to their definitions. Then listen and repeat. TR: 101 and 102

decorative	dramatic	impressive	symbolic

_____ 1. strongly affecting people's emotions

_____ 2. representing something else

_____ 3. useful for making something more attractive

_____ 4. creating a good reaction

6 **Choose an activity.**

1. **Work independently.** Go online to find out more about early paintings in one of the caves you read about. Write a paragraph summarizing what you learned. In your conclusion, say whether you were able to connect to the paintings. Explain why or why not.

2. **Work in pairs.** Create a simple drawing or painting that's symbolic of something in your life. Then, share it with your partner. See if your partner can guess the meaning of your artwork. When you finish, switch roles.

3. **Work in groups.** Choose a modern mural in your community. Compare it with the cave art pictured on pp. 128–129. Consider the medium, technique, and meaning of each piece. Summarize the similarities and differences in a short presentation.

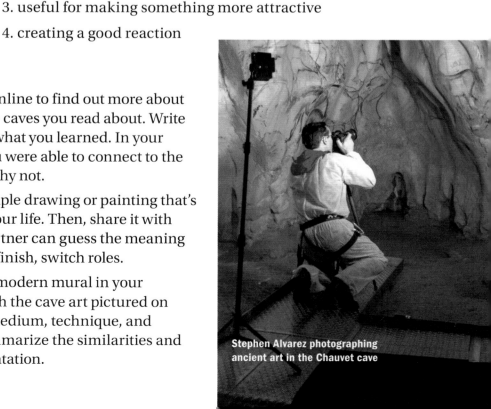

Stephen Alvarez photographing ancient art in the Chauvet cave

Interpreting and expressing understanding

Why did early peoples paint these images on the cave's wall?
> Possibly because <u>they didn't have a writing system</u>.
> It seems to me that <u>it was an expression of religious beliefs</u>.
> It appears that <u>there wasn't much else to do for fun</u>.
> Maybe they did it because <u>they wanted to leave a mark</u>.
> Apparently, <u>people wanted to record their experiences</u>.
> This seems to symbolize/represent <u>their interest in the natural world</u>.

Mayan carvings at Holmul, Guatemala, discovered by National Geographic Explorer Francisco Estrada-Belli and his team

7 **Listen.** How do speakers interpret the artwork? Write the words and phrases you hear. TR: 104

8 **Read and complete the dialogue.**

Carlos: Look at this carved mural, Sylvia. It was discovered in Guatemala. It was preserved in the buried Mayan city of Holmul.

Sylvia: Wow! That's enormous! I wonder why it was so big!

Carlos: _____ the Mayans would usually build new structures on top of older ones, making them bigger.

Sylvia: There are so many different people in the carving. Do you know what they represent?

Carlos: _____ they were Mayan rulers, who were considered gods.

Sylvia: What's that on their heads? Are those birds?

Carlos: Yes. Wearing a headdress made of birds was common in Mayan civilization.
They seem to _____ wealth or power.

Sylvia: _____ of all the brightly colored birds in Guatemala. Their feathers sure did make decorative accessories. And look at this man. Is he holding food?

Carlos: Probably. _____ food was a common offering to the gods.

> It seems to me that the artist had a political message.

9 **Work in groups.** Choose three photos or works of art to share. Put your group's photos into a single pile. Take turns selecting an image from the pile. Then toss the cube. Use the word or phrase on the cube to make a sentence about the image.

Go to p. 173.

10 **Work in pairs.** Choose a photo or a piece of artwork in this book and discuss your interpretations of it.

131

Reported speech: Describing what others say

"This **can't** be an original painting of Georgia O'Keeffe."	He **argued** that it **couldn't be** an original painting of Georgia O'Keeffe.
"Frida Kahlo **had been injured** in a bus accident. After that, she **began** painting."	The teacher **explained** that Frida Kahlo **had been injured** in a bus accident, and **had begun** painting after that.
"We **will begin** studying sculpture later this year."	She **pointed out** that they **would begin** studying sculpture later this year.
"Art **should reflect** the world we live in."	He **suggested** that art **should reflect** the world we live in.
"What exhibition **is** at the art museum this month?"	She **asked** what exhibition **was** at the art museum this month.
"**Go** see Kobra's murals." "You **won't** be disappointed!"	They **told us to go** see Kobra's murals. They **claimed** we **wouldn't** be disappointed.

11 **Read the quotes about art.** Then complete the sentences using reported speech.

"I hate flowers. I paint them because they're cheaper than models and they don't move." —Georgia O'Keeffe

"I paint flowers so they will not die." —Frida Kahlo

"Treat a work of art like a prince. Let it speak to you first." —Arthur Schopenhauer

"The world today doesn't make sense, so why should I paint pictures that do?" —Pablo Picasso

"Art is what you can get away with." —Andy Warhol

"I want to touch people with my art." —Vincent van Gogh

"I don't paint to live, I live to paint." —Willem de Kooning

1. Pablo Picasso stated that _____.

   So he wanted to know _____.

2. Van Gogh explained that _____.

3. Frida Kahlo reflected that _____.

4. Georgia O'Keeffe claimed _____.

   She explained that _____.

5. Arthur Schopenhauer advised us to _____.

People all over the world **admire** Eduardo Kobra's murals. **Critics** compliment his **bold** use of color and attention to detail. Kobra's murals have different **themes**, but many honor the memory of historical figures.

12 **Learn new words.** Listen to an art teacher's lesson on Brazilian street artist Eduardo Kobra. Then listen and repeat. **TR: 106 and 107**

13 **Work in pairs.** Listen again to the lesson. Write what the teacher said. Use reported speech and the words provided. **TR: 108**

1. say / critics / people walking by
She said that Kobra's first critics were people walking by.

2. point out / street art / accept
_____

3. explain / stand out / bold
_____

4. remind / recognize / subject
_____

5. tell / look at / famous
_____

6. ask / choose / favorite
_____

14 **Work in groups.** Think of a mural in your school or community. Compare it to Eduardo Kobra's mural. Talk about the theme, size, technique, level of detail, and use of color. Then take turns explaining to the class what you discussed.

> We pointed out that Kobra used colors that were much bolder than those on the mural in the cafeteria.

133

Microscopic Marvels

Artist Willard Wigan knows how to make a big impression in small places.

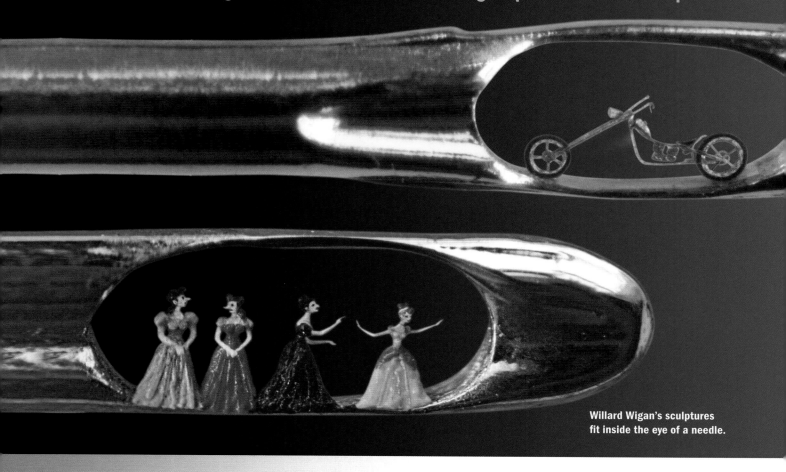

Willard Wigan's sculptures fit inside the eye of a needle.

15 **Before you read, discuss in pairs.** Look at the photo on the right. What do you think this man is doing?

16 **Learn new words.** Find these words in the reading. What do you think they mean? Look at the words that appear right before or after each of the words. Then listen and repeat. TR: 109

detailed	exhibition	to honor
miniature	needle	

17 **While you read, pause after each paragraph.** Write a question you have about Willard Wigan and his work. TR: 110

18 **After you read, work in pairs to respond to the following.**

1. Describe the average size of one of Willard's sculptures.
2. How can you see his work?
3. Who buys it?
4. What materials does he use?
5. What were his first micro-sculptures?

"Just because you can't see something, that doesn't mean it's not there." This old saying is certainly meaningful for British sculptor Willard Wigan. The sculptures he creates are very small, so small that most of them fit on the head of a pin or in the eye of a needle. On average, his works are half the size of the period at the end of this sentence.

People from around the world admire Willard's work (through a microscope, of course!). Celebrities and royalty alike own his sculptures. He's even been honored by the Queen of England for his contributions to the arts. But at every one of his exhibitions, the question is always the same: *How does he do it?*

The answer is very, *very* carefully. So carefully, in fact, that he actually slows his breathing down and works in between breaths. He learned the hard way that he must do this after he once inhaled one of his sculptures.

Before he begins, Willard collects the materials he needs. Many of his sculptures are made with nylon tags from clothing and fibers found in fabrics and carpets around his house. If fibers are too thick, Willard might instead use pieces of a spider web to add detail. To sculpt, Willard works under a microscope using miniature tools that he creates himself. Amazingly, he rarely uses glue. Instead, he carves spaces into the needle or pin, and forms his work so that it fits into those spaces. To paint his sculptures, Willard uses the hair from a dead fly as a paintbrush.

Creating these detailed works is a very long and difficult process, one that Willard admits isn't always the most enjoyable. "It's a nightmare when I start but a dream when I finish," he says. A single sculpture can take up to three months to complete.

People have asked Willard why he has chosen to do something so difficult and time-consuming. His interest in micro-sculpting began when he was five. He started creating houses and playgrounds for ants. Willard was not a strong student. He struggled with dyslexia, and his teachers were quick to call him a failure. This made him feel small, so focusing on little things helped him to feel big. The smaller his work got, the bigger he felt. "I want to show the world that the little things can be the biggest things," he says.

19 **Work in pairs.** Share the questions that you wrote in Activity 17. Then, discuss their answers. Go online to find any answers that weren't in the reading.

20 **Discuss in groups.**

1. Share your reaction to Willard's work and the process he uses to create it.
2. Go online to find additional photos of his sculptures. Share photos with your group members. Describe which ones you like the best.
3. Willard started creating miniature sculptures because his teachers made him feel small, and he wanted to feel big. What makes you feel small? What can you do to change how you feel in this situation?

21 **Before you watch, discuss in pairs.**

1. In this video, you will meet National Geographic Photographer Joel Sartore. What do you think you will learn about him?

2. Many of Joel's photos are of animals. What challenges might he face in trying to get good photos? Name at least two.

22 **Write.** The video you're going to watch is called *A Photographer's Life*. List three things that you think are important in a photographer's life.

1. _____

2. _____

3. _____

23 Watch scene 8.1. **While you watch, listen for the traits that Joel says a photographer needs to have.** Circle the traits you hear.

aggressive	bossy
driven	open-minded
quiet	self-conscious

Joel Sartore with two grizzly bears

24 **After you watch, work in pairs to answer the questions.**

1. What does Joel mean when he says "you can't sleep on it" (in reference to taking photos)?

2. What does Joel seem to dislike about traveling for work?

3. Why do photographers need to quickly establish friendships in new places?

4. How many photos does Joel shoot each year? How many does he think are worth keeping?

5. What is *The Photo Ark*? How long has Joel been working on it?

6. Why is Joel creating *The Photo Ark*?

25 **Work in pairs.** Joel wants people to "look these species in the eye so that they care about these animals more." Why would eye contact make us care more? How do you think eye contact affects relationships between people? Does eye contact have the same effect between animals and people? Explain.

26 **Work in groups.** In the video, Joel says, "Most species are going extinct because we don't pay any attention to them." Give two or three examples of this. Discuss ways to raise awareness of these animals.

27 **Choose an activity.**

1. **Work independently.** Photograph an animal on a plain black or white surface. Show the photo to the class. Tell how and where you took it. Was it easy or difficult? Describe any challenges you faced.

2. **Work in pairs.** Research Joel's project *The Photo Ark*. Choose your favorite five photos. Present them to the class, describing each of the animals.

3. **Work in groups.** Compare and contrast the photography of Joel Sartore and Stephen Alvarez (or another famous photographer). How is their work different? What is the same? Create a Venn diagram to show your comparison.

Two- and three-word verbs

Separable

Artists want to **draw in** their viewers.
Artists want to **draw** their viewers **in**.
Artists want to **draw** us **in**.

I'm working to **track down** the origins of art.
I'm working to **track** the origins of art **down**.
I'm working to **track** them **down**.

Can we **figure out** the meaning of this painting?
Can we **figure** the meaning **out**?
Can we **figure** it **out**?

Inseparable

A true artist **comes up with** unique ways to express herself.

Critics **rave about** the modern art exhibition at the museum. They say it's really impressive!

I'm **looking forward to** seeing the works on display.

Self-Portrait with Bandaged Ear
by Vincent van Gogh, 1889

28 **Read and complete the sentences.** Make any necessary changes. For help, see pp. 149–152.

come up with	cut off	figure out	get away with
look down on	look forward to	take down	track down

1. Vincent van Gogh suffered mental illness, which led him to _____ his ear _____ .

2. Andy Warhol says that "Art is what you can _____ ."

3. Author Robert Edsel is working to _____ works of art that were lost during World War II.

4. One family _____ a Diego Rivera painting _____ and destroyed it because they didn't like the political message.

5. Wealthy Japanese art buyers _____ the technique of woodblock printing used by Katsushika Hokusai. They didn't like making art so accessible.

29 **Work in groups.** Research information for each of the categories on the game board. Then, choose a topic and a verb. Make sentences with the information you researched.

> The Statue of Liberty was supposed to be in Egypt, but instead it ended up in the United States.

	Painting	Famous Artists	Cave Art	Sculpture	Abstract Art
100	FREE	cut off	stand out	fit in	figure out

138

Go to p. 175.

In an art review, you need to give both facts and opinions. Research the artwork and its artist to help you understand the work and the context it was created in. In your review, answer the following questions:

· **What do you see?**

· **How did the artist create the work?**

· **Why did the artist create the work?**

· **What is your reaction to the work?**

30 **Read the model.** Underline the answers to each of the questions above.

The Great Wave off Kanagawa is one of the best-known pieces of art in the world. Japanese artist Katsushika Hokusai created the image sometime around 1830. It was part of a series of thirty-six images to feature Mt. Fuji, Japan's highest mountain. In this image, Mt. Fuji is far off in the background, and looks very small from the viewer's perspective. Fishing boats and their crews are being thrown around by the enormous waves, and viewers can only hope that they get out of the sea unharmed.

The series of images that includes *The Great Wave off Kanagawa* was created on wood blocks. To create the work, Hokusai first drew the image with ink, and then carved it into the wood. Next, colored ink was put on the blocks. Sheets of paper were then pressed onto each of the blocks to print the design. Because Hokusai used this technique to create multiple copies, many people could own this print.

Hokusai had been painting for years before creating this famous print. In fact, he was in his seventies when it came out. He probably chose to feature Mt. Fuji because it is considered a sacred place in Japan. The print method was good for selling art, which may have been another reason why Hokusai created the series.

The Great Wave off Kanagawa is an excellent example of Japanese art. It draws viewers in with its exaggerated movement and interesting perspective. Hokusai uses both Japanese and Western techniques, which gives the print a unique style. The technique makes the art accessible, so that even today, people everywhere can connect with nineteenth-century Japan.

31 **Work in pairs.** What is the author's opinion of the artwork? Do you agree? Why or why not?

32 **Write.** Write a review of a piece of artwork that you've seen in this unit or elsewhere. Be sure to research the work. Include facts and opinions in your review.

Connect Through Art

"We use art as a way to bind society together."

—Stephen Alvarez
National Geographic Photographer

1. Watch scene 8.2.

2. Stephen says that art is a way to "bind society," or connect people together. Think of an example of public art in your community. How does it bring people together?

3. Even if you don't create your own art, you can use art to connect with others. List three ways you can do this.

Make an Impact

A **Hold an art auction.**

· Choose three pieces of art to bring to class.

· Prepare a short description of each piece of art. Talk about the artist, the context in which the artwork was created, and its connection to modern life.

· Hold an art auction for your class. Display each piece and describe it. Try to sell each item to the highest bidder.

B **Create an art book.**

· Research artwork and quotations about artwork. Select five of each.

· Compile the artwork and quotations into a decorative art book.

· Present your book to the class. As you share, explain your connection to the artwork and the quotations.

C **Recreate cave art.**

· Choose a cave that you learned about in this unit, or another cave with prehistoric paintings.

· Research the specific images found on the cave wall. Learn about the medium and the technique used.

· Recreate this art on a piece of cardboard. Present your artwork to the class. Explain what it represents and how you did it. Compare the process to that of the original artists.

Still Life with Apples by Paul Cézanne, 1894

The Houses of Parliament, Sunset by Claude Monet, 1903

Concert of Birds, Circle of Jan van Kessel (Anonymous), 1660/1670

Express Yourself

1 **Read and listen to information about a contest and an entry to the contest.** TR: 112

CALLING ALL CREATIVE TYPES!

Do you have a problem you'd like to solve? Well, come up with a solution!

All Tech Today is sponsoring a contest to help young inventors take a concept and make it a reality.

WINNERS RECEIVE:

- a four-year scholarship for high-tech education
- resources to help build your device
- support in getting your device on the market

To enter, draw a design of your concept. Write an essay to explain your idea and how it's useful.

Droidganizer

Submitted by Alexandra Poulos, age 16

Like most people my age, I hate cleaning up my room. My mom always tells me that if I don't like to do it, I can save my money to buy a robot that will clean up for me. She's joking, of course, but her joke gave me an idea. What if I really *could* get a robot to clean up my room?

As a member of my school's robotics club, I'm learning that it might actually be possible to make, not buy, this robot. My idea, *Droidganizer*, would build on technological devices that already exist to help around the house. Currently, there are robotic devices that vacuum and mop the floor using sensors to control their movement. Robots also have the ability to pick things up with robotic limbs. *Droidganizer* would combine these applications into a single device.

What would really set *Droidganizer* apart from current devices is its monitor. A *Droidganizer* owner would put the monitor on the ceiling somewhere in the room. The person would clean and tidy the room the first time, and then use the monitor to take a photo of how the room should look. The monitor would store this information. Then, it would monitor the room from the ceiling. Whenever the room doesn't match the photo, *Droidganizer* would automatically fix the problem. It would pick up clothes or books on the floor and put them away. It might also make the bed. *Droidganizer* could even be programmed to vacuum, dust, or clean the windows!

Anyone would be happy to have a *Droidganizer* to do the dirty work. If only *Droidganizer* existed now! People could be using their time studying, playing sports, or hanging out with friends—not cleaning!

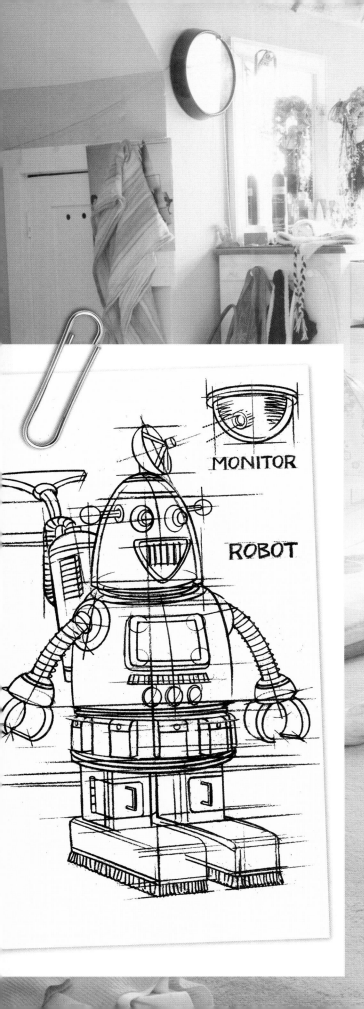

MONITOR

ROBOT

2 **Discuss in pairs.**

1. You just read about a device that would solve a problem. Do you think the concept presented is unique? Should Alexandra's entry be considered for the contest? Explain.

2. What steps do you think are involved in inventing and selling a product like *Droidganizer*? List at least five. Then compare your list with another pair.

3. Why do you think the contest organizers asked for a design? How can the design be useful in helping them connect with the idea?

3 **Connect ideas.** In Unit 7, you learned about creative problem-solving. In Unit 8, you learned about art connections. What connection do you see between the two units?

4 **Choose an activity.**

1. Choose a topic:
   - creative problem-solving
   - art connections

2. Choose a way to express yourself:
   - a magazine article
   - an entry for an art or technology contest
   - a short video

3. Present your work.

Unit 1

Intonation in embedded *yes/no* questions

1 **Listen.** Notice how the voice falls at the end of the statement and rises at the end of a question with a *yes* or *no* answer. TR: 113

Statement: Cory Richards is a photographer.

Yes/No question: Is Cory a climber?

If a *yes/no* question is embedded, however, the intonation depends *not* on the question, but on the sentence with the embedded question. If the sentence is a statement, the voice falls at the end. If it's a *yes/no* question, the voice rises at the end.

I wonder if Cory is a climber.

Do you know if Cory is a climber?

2 **Listen and repeat.** Write an up or down arrow to indicate the final intonation. TR: 114

1. I wonder if he's ever surfed. _____
2. Do you know if she has a role model? _____
3. I'm not sure if he's achieved a goal. _____
4. Are you asking if he's reached his limit? _____

3 **Work in pairs.** Take turns completing the two embedded questions for each item using *I wonder if he/she . . .* and *Do you know if he/she . . . ?*

I wonder if she's <u>ever surfed</u>.　　Do you know if she's <u>ever surfed</u>?

1. Has she ever surfed?
2. Does he have a hobby?
3. Does she take many risks?
4. Has he overcome an obstacle?

Unit 2

Stress in compound nouns

1 **Listen.** Notice the stress in these compound nouns. TR: 115

A *compound noun* is formed when two words come together to form a single noun.

crowdsourcing　　**earth**quake
cell phone　　**fund**raiser
text message　　**sea** level

The first word in most compound nouns receives the main stress. This differs from adjective plus noun combinations, where the second word usually receives the main stress.

This is a good **phone**.　　What's the best **date**?
This is a **cell** phone.　　What's the **up**date?

2 **Listen and repeat.** Circle the word with the main stress. TR: 116

1. a **lap**top
2. a loud call
3. the hard work
4. daytime
5. a nice top
6. a phone call
7. the homework
8. good time

3 **Work in pairs.** Take turns reading the clues aloud. For each clue, your partner will say the compound noun.

work you do at home　　**home**work

1. work you do at home
2. a computer that sits on your lap
3. another student from your class
4. another word for *soccer*
5. food from the ocean

Unit 3

The letter *t* between vowels

1 Listen. Notice the pronunciation of the letter *t* in these words and phrases. **TR: 117**

attitude   eating   a **lot** of
butter   **mat**ters   **got** to

In North American English, the letter *t* can sound like a quick *d*. This happens when *t* is between two vowels and the first vowel is stressed, but the one after it is unstressed. Listen again.

If the syllable after the letter *t* is stressed, then it sounds like a *t*. Listen to the examples.

attend   eighteen   a table

2 Listen and repeat. Circle three more underlined letters where the *t* sounds like the *t* in *table*. **TR: 118**

attack   eat it   monitor crops
butter   protein source grow tomatoes
big city   polluted land   fresh water

3 Work in pairs. Listen and repeat. Then take turns asking and answering the questions about Unit 3. Use the page numbers if you need help. The underlined *t*'s sound like a quick *d*. **TR: 119**

1. Who took tomatoes and potatoes to Europe? (p. 49)
2. According to Barton, what is a good protein source? (p. 49)
3. How does the water supply become polluted? (p. 51)
4. What does the title *Grow It Here, Eat It Here* refer to? (pp. 50–51)
5. Why is eating insects a good idea? (pp. 52–53)

Unit 4

Expressing emotions with intonation

1 Listen. Notice the different possible emotions in the responses. **TR: 120**

A: There's a new amusement park nearby!
B1: That's great! (enthusiastic/excited)
B2: That's great. (sarcastic/annoyed/ not interested)
B3: That's great? (questioning/doubtful)

Speakers use intonation in various ways to express emotions. Listen again. Notice how the voice is sometimes higher and sometimes lower.

Generally, a speaker's voice becomes higher when the speaker is positive (happy, excited, enthusiastic) and lower when negative (angry, annoyed, sarcastic).

2 Listen. Circle the responses with an excited emotion. **TR: 121**

1. —The Olympics will be here.   —Awesome.
2. —The water is recycled.   —That's great.
3. —I got you a ticket to the park.   —Thank you.
4. —Look at that roller coaster.   —Wow.
5. —He became president.   —Interesting.

The Olympics will be here!   Awesome!

3 Work in pairs. Take turns saying the sentences in Activity 2. Respond with one of the two emotions. Circle your partner's emotion.

1. Awesome.   a. sarcastic   b. excited
2. That's great.   a. questioning   b. enthusiastic
3. Thank you.   a. annoyed   b. questioning
4. Wow.   a. sarcastic   b. excited
5. Interesting.   a. excited   b. doesn't care

Unit 5

Sounds of letter x

1 **Listen.** Notice the pronunciation of the letter x. TR: 122

ks	gz
ex**plore**	ex**act**
Mexico	ex**ist**

The letter x can be pronounced two ways—ks or gz. The pronunciation is usually ks. However, when the x comes before a vowel **and** the syllable after x is stressed, the x sounds like gz.

Note: There are a few words that begin with x (xylophone). In this case, the x sounds like z.

2 **Listen and repeat.** Then write ks or gz to indicate the sound of x. TR: 123

1. __ks__ explore
2. _____ expert
3. _____ executive
4. _____ exercise
5. _____ exam
6. _____ complex
7. _____ exist
8. _____ exactly

3 **Work in pairs.** Complete the paragraph with the words. Then listen and check your answers. Take turns reading the paragraph with your partner. TR: 124

exactly	exciting	existence	expedition	experience
explore	Mexican	Mexico	taxes	

Come __explore__ _____! Our _____ is led by an _____ in _____ history. In your fascinating ten-day _____, you will learn about the _____ of prehistoric civilizations.

The cost of this _____ trip is _____ $3,000. No _____ or added fees. Book today!

Unit 6

Pausing: Relative clauses

1 **Listen.** Notice the pauses in these relative clauses. TR: 125

Dinosaurs,/ **which were reptiles,**/ are the ancestors of birds.

Reptiles **that flew in prehistoric times** were not dinosaurs.

Herbivores,/ **which don't eat meat,** /can be very large animals.

An animal **that eats meat** is a carnivore.

In writing, commas often indicate a pause. If the relative clause does not have a comma, there's no pause.

2 **Listen and repeat.** Add a comma if you hear a pause before and after the relative clause. TR: 126

1. Elephants and moose, **which are herbivores,** are large land animals.
2. The moose **that ran in front of the car** is OK.
3. Catalina Pimiento **who is a scientist** studies sharks.
4. Great white sharks scare people **who swim or surf.**
5. Nizar Ibrahim studies *Spinosaurus* **which was a prehistoric river monster.**

3 **Listen.** Notice the pauses. Listen again and read the sentences with the speaker. TR: 127

1. *Spinosaurus,* which lived around 97 million years ago, was huge. It had massive teeth that were razor sharp.
2. *T. rex,* which many believe was the largest dinosaur, was smaller than *Spinosaurus. T. rex* had a long tail that was very heavy.

Unit 7

Variations in stress and intonation

1 **Listen.** Notice the stress and intonation differences in the pair of sentences. TR: 128

The invention is **really great**.

The invention is **really great**.

The stress on the adverb *really* is stronger in the second example. The speaker emphasizes it to express a stronger belief. The vowel is longer, and the speaker's voice rises.

Speakers also emphasize words when:

- contrasting information
- correcting information
- stating new information

2 **Listen and repeat.** Circle the syllable with stronger emphasis. TR: 129

1. **Wow. This drone flies (so) high.**
2. **Wow. This drone flies so high.**
3. A: It was a **great ide**a.
   B: It was an **awful ide**a.
4. A: **Jane won** the **science con**test.
   B: **Tim won** the **science con**test.
5. A: You **love robo**tics?
   B: Yes, **micro robo**tics.

3 **Work in pairs.** Take turns saying the sentences in Activity 2. Discuss the meaning of the special emphasis in each sentence or dialogue.

Wow. This drone flies SO high.

The speaker can't believe how high the drone flies. It's very high.

Unit 8

Stress with two- and three-word verbs

1 **Listen.** Notice the stress in these sentences. TR: 130

I **figured out** the **mea**ning.

I **figured** the **mea**ning **out**.

I **figured** it **out**.

In separable two-word verbs, both words are stressed. The object is also stressed except when it's a pronoun.

Notice the stress in these sentences.

She **puts up** with the **noise**.

She **puts up** with it.

In three-word verbs, the third word (*with*) is a preposition. Prepositions are not usually stressed. The first two words as well as the object are stressed, unless the object is a pronoun.

2 **Listen and repeat.** Tap your finger as you say the stressed syllables. TR: 131

1. I can't **figure out** the **mea**ning.
2. A: She **came up** with a **great idea**.
   B: How did she **come up** with it?
3. A: Did you **track down** the **own**ers?
   B: No, I couldn't **track** them **down**.
4. A: Why did van Gogh **cut** his **ear off**?
   B: I didn't know that he **cut** it **off**.

3 **Work in pairs.** Listen and repeat these questions. Then ask and answer them with your partner. TR: 132

Who **cut off** his **ear**?

Van Gogh.

1. Who **cut off** his **ear**?
2. If your friends are sad, how do you **cheer** them **up**?
3. What do you use to **look up** infor**ma**tion?
4. What is something that you **look for**ward to?

Irregular Verbs

Infinitive	Simple past	Past participle	Infinitive	Simple past	Past participle
be	were	been	leave	left	left
beat	beat	beaten	lend	lent	lent
become	became	become	let	let	let
begin	began	begun	lie (down)	lay	lain
bend	bent	bent	light	lit	lit
bet	bet	bet	lose	lost	lost
bite	bit	bitten	make	made	made
bleed	bled	bled	mean	meant	meant
blow	blew	blown	meet	met	met
break	broke	broken	overcome	overcame	overcome
bring	brought	brought	pay	paid	paid
build	built	built	put	put	put
burn	burned/burnt	burned/burnt	quit	quit	quit
buy	bought	bought	read	read	read
carry	carried	carried	ride	rode	ridden
catch	caught	caught	ring	rang	rung
choose	chose	chosen	rise	rose	risen
come	came	come	run	ran	run
cost	cost	cost	say	said	said
cut	cut	cut	see	saw	seen
deal	dealt	dealt	sell	sold	sold
dig	dug	dug	send	sent	sent
dive	dove/dived	dived	set	set	set
do	did	done	sew	sewed	sewn
draw	drew	drawn	shake	shook	shaken
drink	drank	drunk	shine	shone	shone
drive	drove	driven	show	showed	shown
dry	dried	dried	shrink	shrank	shrunk
eat	ate	eaten	shut	shut	shut
fall	fell	fallen	sing	sang	sung
feed	fed	fed	sink	sank	sunk
feel	felt	felt	sit	sat	sat
fight	fought	fought	sleep	slept	slept
find	found	found	slide	slid	slid
flee	fled	fled	speak	spoke	spoken
fly	flew	flown	spend	spent	spent
forbid	forbade	forbidden	spin	spun	spun
forget	forgot	forgotten	stand	stood	stood
forgive	forgave	forgiven	steal	stole	stolen
freeze	froze	frozen	stick	stuck	stuck
fry	fried	fried	sting	stung	stung
get	got	gotten	stink	stank	stunk
give	gave	given	strike	struck	struck/stricken
go	went	gone	swear	swore	sworn
grind	ground	ground	sweep	swept	swept
grow	grew	grown	swim	swam	swum
hang	hung	hung	swing	swung	swung
have	had	had	take	took	taken
hear	heard	heard	teach	taught	taught
hide	hid	hidden	tear	tore	torn
hit	hit	hit	tell	told	told
hold	held	held	think	thought	thought
hurt	hurt	hurt	throw	threw	thrown
keep	kept	kept	understand	understood	understood
kneel	knelt/kneeled	knelt/kneeled	wake	woke	woken
knit	knitted/knit	knitted/knit	wear	wore	worn
know	knew	known	weave	wove/weaved	woven/weaved
lay	laid	laid	win	won	won
lead	led	led	write	wrote	written

Two-word Verbs – Inseparable

Verb	Meaning	Sample sentence
amount to	be the same as; turn out to be	The total **amounts to** five hundred. Some people thought he would not **amount to** anything, but he became famous.
apply for	to make a request	Do you plan to **apply for** a summer job?
apply to	be relevant	The rules **apply to** everyone!
ask around	ask several people	I'll **ask around** in case anyone found a lost phone.
break down	stop functioning	The car **broke down** yesterday.
break up	end a relationship	Did you hear that Lara and Renato **broke up**?
calm down	relax after being angry	**Calm down**! Everything will be OK.
check in	register at a hotel or airport	We can't **check in** until one o'clock.
check out	leave a hotel	He **checked out** at 10:20 and went straight to the airport.
cheer up	become happier	**Cheer up**! I'm sure your team will do better next time.
come across	find unexpectedly	I **came across** a very interesting article about crocodiles.
come from	originate in	Mangoes originally **come from** Asia.
count on	rely on	Please be there on time. I'm **counting on** you!
dress up	wear nice clothes	Mom, do I really need to **dress up** for the party?
eat out	eat at a restaurant	Why don't we **eat out** on Friday?
end up	eventually do/decide	We **ended up** going to the movies last night.
engage in	take part in	The principal **engaged in** talks with the student council.
fall apart	break into pieces	Mom, I need a new desk. This one's **falling apart**.
fall down	fall to the ground	I **fell down** and broke my ankle!
find out	learn	I was so excited when I **found out** we were going to Spain!
fit in	blend in; belong because you're similar	Teenagers wear certain clothes to **fit in**.
get along	be friendly with someone	I really like Tom. We **get along** well.
get over	recover from a problem	I know she's upset you didn't call her, but she'll **get over** it.
get together	meet; gather	Let's **get together** on Wednesday after school!
get up	get out of bed; rise	I **get up** at seven o'clock every day.
give in	surrender; quit	I won't **give in** to pressure from my friends.
give up	stop trying	Don't **give up**. This puzzle is too hard.
go ahead	do; begin to do	Why don't you **go ahead** and invite her to the party?
go back	return	He **went back** to the site and discovered a second dinosaur.
go over	review	Let's **go over** the presentation before class.
grow up	become an adult	I **grew up** in China.
hang in	stay positive	**Hang in** there. I'm sure you'll find the phone.
hang on	wait	**Hang on** a minute. I'm on the phone.
hang out	spend time	Do you want to **hang out** on Saturday?
hold on	wait	**Hold on** a second! I think I found the answer.
lead to	cause to happen	His research **led to** the discovery of a new species.

Verb	Meaning	Sample sentence
light up	become bright	The sky **lit up** with fireworks.
log in/on	sign in to a website or app	I can't **log in** because I don't remember my password.
look after	take care of	I have to **look after** my little sister this Sunday.
look back	think about things that happened in the past	**Looking back,** I think the other project topic was more interesting.
look for	try to find	What are you **looking for**? Did you lose anything?
look into	try to find out about	I need to **look into** it. I'll let you know tomorrow.
not care for	not like	I do**n't** really **care for** opera.
pass away	die	I heard Kim's grandma **passed away**.
prey on	hunt and kill for food	Do lions **prey on** zebras?
rave about	talk or write very enthusiastically	Critics are **raving about** the new film.
rely on	trust; depend on	Do you think we **rely on** technology too much?
run away	escape; leave	Our dog **ran away**!
run into	meet unexpectedly; collide	Yesterday I **ran into** my first grade teacher. I **ran into** a tree.
stand out	be noticeable	I was the only one wearing purple. I really **stood out**.
take off	start to fly	The flight **took off** on time.
turn out	result; happen	I thought everyone in my family had a cell phone. It **turns out** my uncle refuses to get one!
wake up	stop sleeping	I usually **wake up** at six o'clock.
warm up	prepare for exercise	Do you **warm up** before soccer games?
work out	be successful; exercise	Everyone liked our presentation. It **worked out** well! I prefer to **work out** in the gym when it's cold.

Two-word Verbs – Separable

Verb	Meaning	Sample sentence
back up	support	His friends **backed** him **up**.
call off	cancel	They had planned a party, but they had to **call** it **off**.
calm down	help relax	Let's play soft music to **calm** the baby **down**.
carry out	do or complete something	They are **carrying out** research on ancient birds.
check out	observe; notice	**Check out** my new phone!
cheer up	try to make someone happy	Why don't we get some flowers to **cheer** her **up**?
clean up	organize; clean	Can you **clean** that **up**? Guests are arriving soon.
cut down	make something fall to the ground	They're **cutting down** too many trees.
cut off	remove by cutting	Did you read about that hiker that had to **cut off** his own arm?
do over	do again	My brother spilled soda on my poster, so I had to **do** it **over**!
draw in	capture the interest	This book really **drew** me **in**.
equip with	supply with	They **equipped** the astronauts **with** extra oxygen tanks.
figure out	find the answer; solve	He finally **figured** it **out**.
fill out	write information in a form	Remember to **fill out** the form before the end of the week.

Verb	Meaning	Sample sentence
fill up	fill to the top	Don't **fill up** the cup. I need room for milk.
find out	discover information	How did you **find** that **out**?
get across	make understandable	We need to add more examples to **get** the idea **across**!
give back	return something	Do you still have my book? Can you **give** it **back** to me?
give up	quit (a habit)	I'm **giving up** coffee!
hand in	submit	Did you **hand in** the homework in time?
hand out	distribute	I'll make copies and **hand** them **out**.
let down	disappoint	I really want you to come to the party. Don't **let** me **down**.
let in	allow to come in	They didn't **let** him **in** with his backpack.
light up	make bright	At night the stars **light** the sky **up**.
look up	find information	Can you **look** it **up** in a dictionary?
make up	lie about; invent	That can't be true. I think he **made** it **up**.
mix up	confuse things or people	They always **mix** me **up** with my sister.
put off	postpone	Can we **put off** the meeting until next week?
put together	assemble	Can you help me **put** this **together**?
take down	remove	They **took down** the painting because it was controversial.
take off	remove	**Take off** that coat. You'll be too hot.
take over	gain control of	He **took over** the company when his father died.
throw away	put in the garbage; get rid of	Don't **throw away** plastic bottles. Recycle them.
track down	find after a long search	I'm trying to **track down** a friend from first grade.
try on	put on to see if it fits	I **tried on** my sister's shoes, but they didn't fit.
turn away	reject; refuse to admit	He applied to ten schools, but eight **turned** him **away**.
turn down	decrease the strength	**Turn** the TV **down** a bit. It's too loud.
turn off	power off	Don't forget to **turn off** the lights when you leave.
turn on	power on	**Turn on** the TV. The game has started!
turn up	increase the strength	I can't hear. Can you **turn up** the volume?
warm up	make warmer	Can you **warm up** the milk?
work out	find a solution	I'm sure you'll **work** it **out**.

Three-word Verbs – Inseparable

Verb	Meaning	Sample sentence
add up to	become a certain amount; result in something	The total **adds up to** two hundred.
break up with	end a relationship	She **broke up with** her boyfriend last week.
come down with	get sick	He **came down with** a cold.
come up against	face; confront	He **came up against** many obstacles during his research.
come up with	think of; find a solution	She **came up with** an excellent plan.
cut down on	use less of; do less	You should **cut down on** so much screen time!
get along with	be friendly with	My sister **gets along with** everyone!
get around to	find time to finally do	I finally **got around to** writing holiday cards.
get away with	not get caught	How did you **get away with** not doing the homework?
get back into	become interested again	I stopped playing soccer two years ago, but then I **got back into** it.

Verb	Meaning	Sample sentence
get out of	avoid doing something you don't want to do	I think that's just an excuse to **get out of** doing the project!
give up on	lose hope that somebody or something will succeed	I **gave up on** trying to become an athlete.
grow out of	change your mind over time; become too big for	He wants to be a rock star, but I'm sure he'll **grow out of** it. You'll **grow out of** that jacket before winter is over!
look down on	feel that somebody is less important	Many people **looked down on** him and his art, but he went on to become a famous artist.
look forward to	be excited about (something in the future)	I **look forward to** going on vacation.
look out for	protect; take care of	He's very selfish! He only **looks out for** himself.
look up to	have a lot of respect for	Many kids **look up to** athletes or pop stars.
play around with	try several options	I **played around with** it until I found the problem!
put up with	tolerate	Our teacher doesn't **put up with** bad behavior.
run out of	use everything	I think we've **run out of** milk. Can you get some?
stand up for	defend	Don't let him make fun of you. **Stand up for** yourself!
watch out for	be alert; anticipate	**Watch out for** deer crossing the road!

Verbs followed by infinitives and gerunds

Verbs followed by infinitive			Verbs followed by infinitive or noun/pronoun + infinitive		Verbs followed by noun/pronoun + infinitive	
He **agreed to go**.			He **wants to learn** French. I **want him to learn** French.		I **convinced her to try** sushi.	
afford	deserve	offer	ask	prepare	cause	motivate
agree	fail	plan	choose	promise	challenge	order
appear	happen	pretend	dare	want	convince	persuade
arrange	hesitate	refuse	expect	wish	empower	remind
attempt	hope	seem	need	would like	forbid	tell
care	intend	tend			force	urge
claim	learn	vow			hire	warn
decide	manage	wait			invite	
demand						

Verbs followed by gerund or noun/pronoun + infinitive	Verbs followed by a gerund				
They don't **allow surfing** here. They didn't **allow him to surf** here.	You should **avoid swimming** there.				
advise	admit	delay	imagine	mind	report
allow	anticipate	deny	involve	miss	resist
encourage	appreciate	discuss	justify	postpone	risk
permit	avoid	dislike	keep	practice	suggest
require	can't help	enjoy	look forward to	put off	understand
	carry on	feel like	mention	recommend	
	consider	finish			

Verbs followed by infinitive or gerund (similar meaning)			Verbs followed by infinitive or gerund (different meaning)	
I **hate waking** up early. I **hate to wake** up early.			I **remember going** there last year. I **remembered to go** to the store.	
begin	hate	prefer	forget	remember
can't bear	like	propose	go on	stop
can't stand	love	start	quit	try
continue			regret	

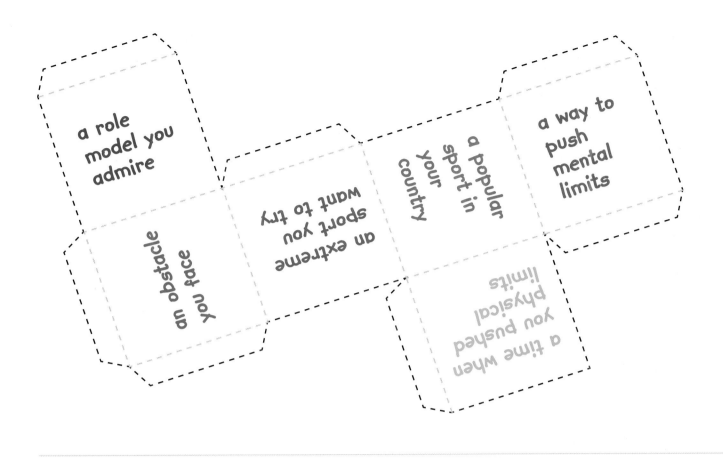

a role model you admire

an obstacle you face

an extreme sport you want to try

a popular sport in your country

a way to push mental limits

a time when you pushed physical limits

Donate money

Become a digital humanitarian

Volunteer with a rescue organization

agree

disagree

Travel to a disaster area to help

Organize a fundraiser

Ask for help using social media

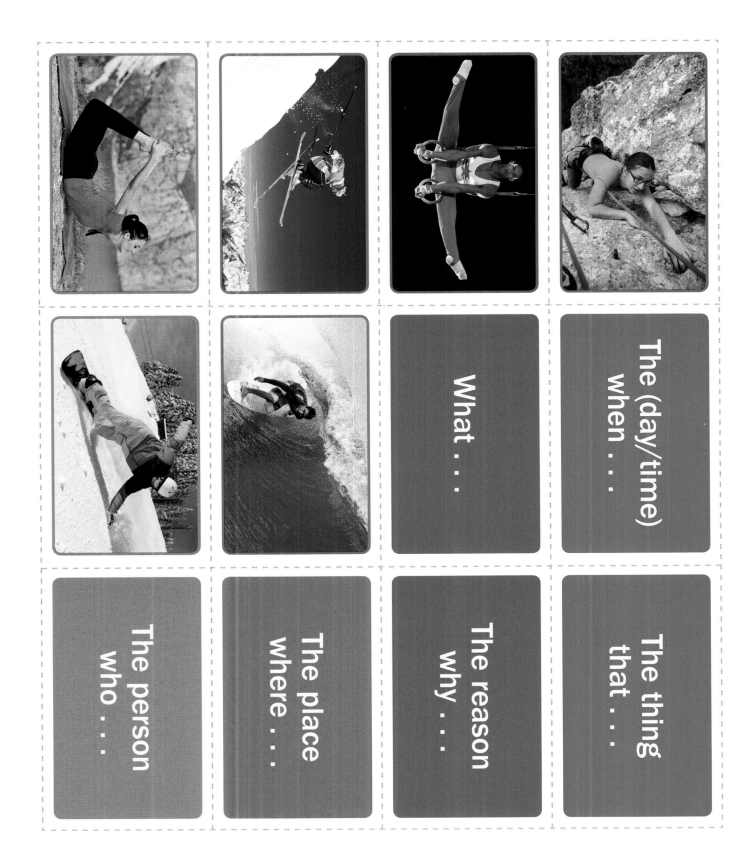

What . . .

The (day/time)
when . . .

The person
who . . .

The place
where . . .

The reason
why . . .

The thing
that . . .

	Technology	People	The world	School	Transportation
100	computers	live	people	homework	bicycles
200	television	buy	country	classrooms	cars
300	cell phones	work	environment	computers	airplanes
400	games	have	population	teachers	space travel
500	radio	eat	problem	classes	trains

Unit 3 Cutouts Use with Activity 9 on p. 47.

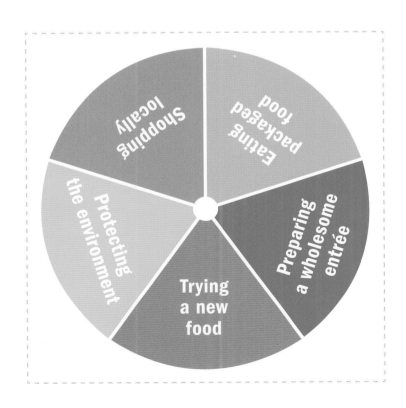

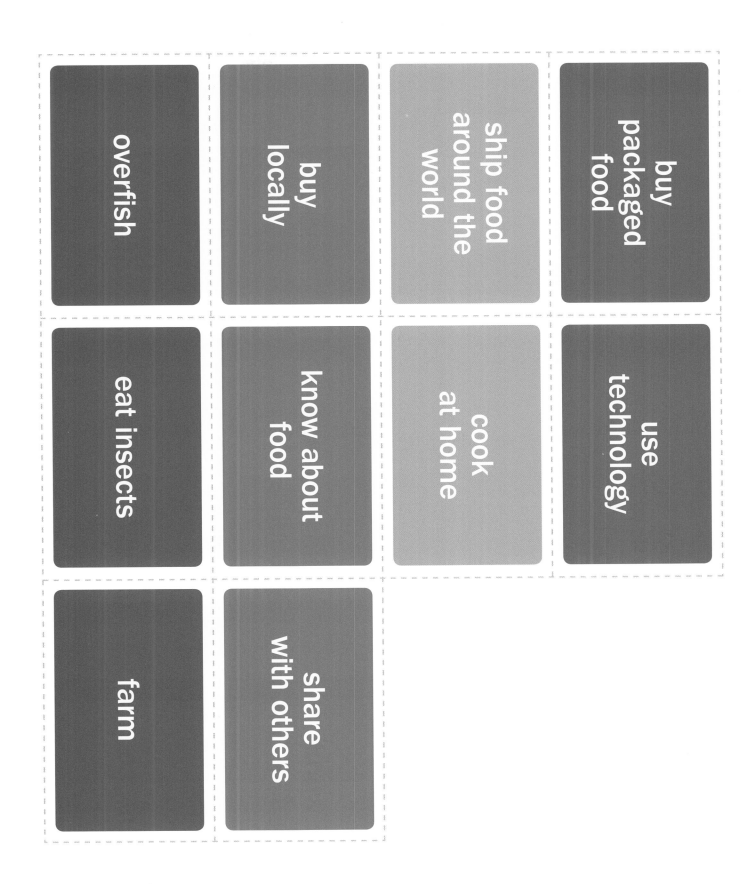

overfish

buy locally

ship food around the world

buy packaged food

eat insects

know about food

cook at home

use technology

farm

share with others

Begin by saying:

Concerts aren't harmful to the environment. People are just there to hear the music.

Correct by saying:

Only 1 in 5 water bottles gets recycled.

Begin by saying:

You don't need reusable bags for shopping. You can just get plastic bags from the store.

Correct by saying:

Air shows are popular all over the world. Each year, about 600 shows are performed.

Begin by saying:

Air shows can have a negative impact, but they happen so rarely that it isn't a big problem.

Correct by saying:

Many amusement parks use high-efficiency LED lights.

Begin by saying:

Buying bottled water isn't bad for the environment. You just need to recycle the bottles.

Correct by saying:

A single auto race uses almost 20,000 l (5,300 gal.) of fuel.

Begin by saying:

Car racing isn't that bad for the environment. The races are over so fast, they can't possibly use too much fuel.

Correct by saying:

Around 1 trillion plastic bags are consumed each year. Plastic bags can take nearly 1,000 years to break down.

Begin by saying:

Amusement parks use too much energy to light up their rides.

Correct by saying:

People litter at concerts. For example, over 1,600 tons of garbage were left after a single concert in the United Kingdom.

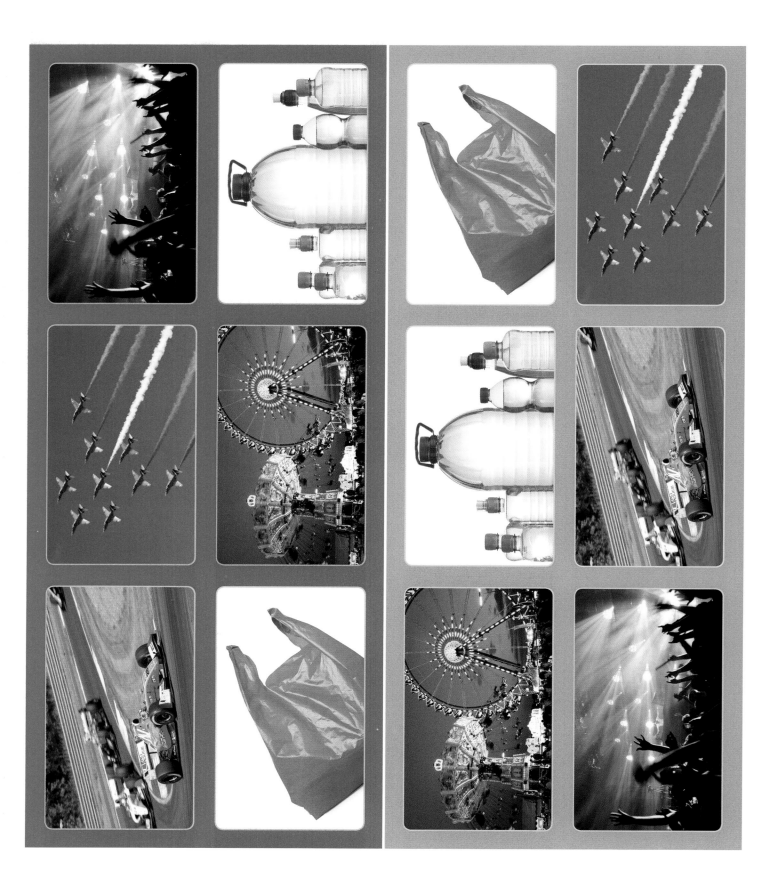

START

Find a venue that's accessible by bus. (think about)

Advertise with social media, not paper. (continue)

Sell packaged food. (avoid)

Invite environmental non-profits. (recommend)

There's too much litter to clean up. **LOSE A TURN!**

Great job! You found ways to refill water containers. **MOVE AHEAD 3 SPACES!**

Use plastic water bottles. (stop)

You suggest selling bottled water. **GO BACK TO START!**

THE EVENT WAS A SUCCESS! CONGRATULATIONS! END

Reuse items from other events. (recommend)

Use recycled paper for posters. (choose)

If you could go anywhere in the world, where would you go?

Would you want to travel to an extreme place, such as the ocean floor? Why or why not?

Why do humans explore?

Which explorer that you've learned about interests you the most? Why?

Identify an explorer of the past. Where did he/she go? What did he/she discover?

What can we learn about ourselves when we go to new places?

Do you have an explorer in your family? Who is it? Where has this person gone?

Would you want to live and study in another country for a year? Why or why not?

If you hosted a student from another country, what would you show him/her?

What obstacles must people overcome to explore new places?

What was the most exciting place you've ever explored? Why?

Would you consider yourself an explorer? Why or why not?

Eugenie
Clark

Annie
Smith Peck

Amelia
Earhart

Mary
Kingsley

Lee
Berger

Barrington
Irving

Sylvia
Earle

Corey
Jaskolski

travel
Africa
Sierra Leone
Gabon
Ogowe River

fly solo
Atlantic Ocean
Canada
Ireland

climb
Huascarán
Andes
Peru

study sharks
South Pacific Ocean
Sea of Cortez
Mexico

film King Tut's tomb
Egypt
Middle East

lead team of aquanauts
Atlantic Ocean
Bahamas

fly solo
Jamaica
Miami
United States

discover fossils
South Africa
Johannesburg
Southern Hemisphere

The paleontologist who researches *Spinosaurus* is Nizar Ibrahim.

Great white sharks, who are underwater hunters, can smell a drop of blood up to 5 km (3 mi.) away.

The manta rays that live in the waters of the Indian Ocean have the largest brain of any fish.

Steve Sillett, who is a giant tree specialist, estimates the President is one of the fastest-growing trees in the world.

Blue whales have enormous tongues that weigh as much as an elephant.

The *T. rex*, which was the fiercest land predator of its time, had huge jaws and teeth.

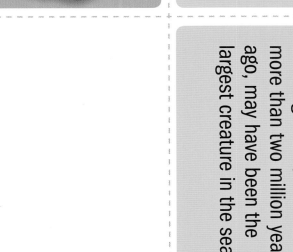

Rafflesia, which are found in Indonesia, are giant flowers measuring over 1 m (3.3 ft.) wide.

The megalodon, which lived more than two million years ago, may have been the largest creature in the sea.

really

so

hardly

rather

very

kind of

Kenneth Shinozuka
created sensors to help
his grandfather and other
Alzheimer's patients.

Richard Turere's
invention protected
his family's cattle
from lions.

Kelvin Doe became
a DJ by creating his own
radio equipment.

Deepika Kurup invented
a solar-powered device
that cleans water.

Tan Le helps
researchers study the
brain with her Emotiv
Insight headset.

Sanga Moses brings
clean energy to people
in Uganda.

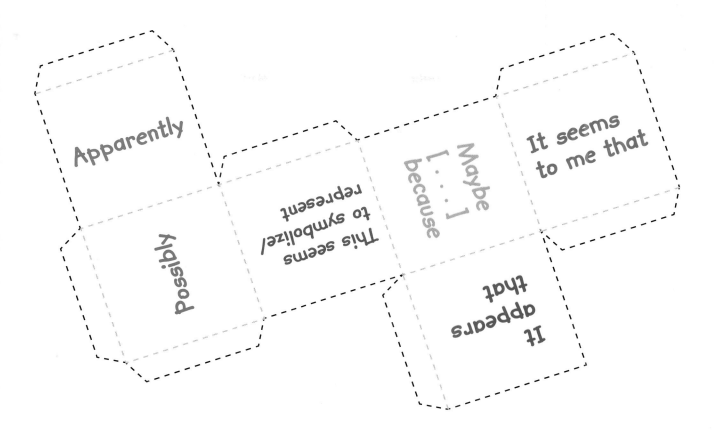

	Painting	Famous Artists	Cave Art	Sculpture	Abstract Art
100	FREE	cut off	stand out	fit in	figure out
200	hang up	FREE	figure out	put together	look down on
300	track down	give up on	FREE	get across	come up with
400	calm down	throw away	draw in	FREE	give up on
500	put up with	come up against	let (us) in on	rave about	FREE

Seattle fans and fireworks were flying high at Qwest Field after the 34-14 win over the Carolina Panthers in the NFC Championship game that sent the Seahawks to the Super Bowl. With a 13-3 regular-season record and two playoff victories, it was the best Seahawks season in the 30-year history of the team.

The Seattle Times

seattletimes.com

This book is available in quantity at special discounts for your group or organization.
For further information, contact:

Triumph Books
542 South Dearborn Street, Suite 750
Chicago, Illinois 60605
Phone: 312-939-3330 • Fax: 312-663-3557

Printed in the United States of America

TRIUMPH
BOOKS

CHICAGO

Super Seahawks

THE STORY OF THE SEAHAWKS' MAGICAL RUN TO THE SUPER BOWL

CONTENTS

ON THE COVER:

Matt Hasselbeck holds up the George Halas trophy, given to the winner of the NFC Championship.

PHOTOGRAPHS:

Rod Mar: Front and back covers; Pages 2-4, 12, 14-15, 19, 22-23, 24 (bottom), 26-29, 30 (top), 32-33, 35 (left and bottom right), 44-46, 48-55, 56 (top), 57-59, 61-71, 74-82, 86-89, 91, 92, 93 (bottom), 95-97, 99,100 (bottom), 102-105, 107, 108 (top and bottom right), 109, 115 (bottom), 116, 117, 120, 121 (bottom left and center), 122, 124-126, 128

Dean Rutz: Pages 5, 9, 11, 13, 20, 24 (top), 25, 30 (bottom), 34, 35 (top right), 36, 37, 38 (bottom), 56 (bottom), 90, 91 (top), 93 (top), 108 (bottom left), 110-113, 121 (right)

John Lok: Pages 7 (top), 8, 21, 38 (top), 39, 60, 85, 100 (top), 101

Mike Siegel: Pages 1, 6, 7 (bottom), 31, 40-43

Jim Bates: Pages 72-73, 83-84, 115 (top), 121 (top)

Steve Ringman: Page 17

Dustin Snipes: Page 47

3

MOTOWN LETDOWN

Seahawks brought down by mistakes, penalties and three Steelers plays

BY STEVE KELLEY
Seattle Times staff columnist

The Seahawks did so much this season. More than any other team in franchise history. They won 13 games, 11 in a row at one point. They won the NFC Championship for the first time. Shaun Alexander won the rushing title and was the league's MVP. Seven players invited to the Pro Bowl. But in their final game, a game that will be remembered for its lack of artistry, the better team didn't win Super Bowl XL. The Seahawks lost, 21-10. ➤

Shaun Alexander (left) was the top rusher in the game with 95 yards.

Seattle scores first on this 47-yard field goal by Josh Brown (right) in the first quarter.

4

STEELERS
21
SEAHAWKS
10

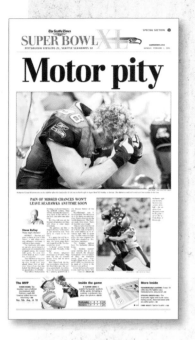

> " The bottom line, we just stalled out in the red zone. We were moving the ball fine, had rhythm, time of possession, first downs; we just didn't score touchdowns" — QUARTERBACK MATT HASSELBECK

SCORING

Seattle	3	0	7	0	10
Pittsburgh	0	7	7	7	21

HAWK HIGHLIGHTS

QB Matt Hasselbeck:
26-49, 273 yards, TD, IN

RB Shaun Alexander:
20 carries, 95 yards

WR Joe Jurevicius:
5 catches, 93 yards

WR Darrell Jackson:
5 catches, 50 yards, all in the first quarter

CB Kelly Herndon:
76-yard interception return, longest in Super Bowl history

BY THE NUMBERS

7-70—Seahawks penalties and yards lost
3-20—Steelers penalties and yards lost

SEAHAWK SURPRISE

Seattle had 396 total yards compared to Pittsburgh's 339. The Seahawks had possession of the ball for 33:02 compared to the Steelers' 26:58.

Seahawks Darrell Jackson and Steelers Chris Hope face off after Jackson's apparent touchdown in the first quarter was nullified by a pass-interference penalty on Jackson.

Seahawks linebacker Lofa Tatupu brings down Steelers quarterback Ben Roethlisberger in the first quarter. Tatupu led the Seattle defense with nine tackles.

➤ "It hurts," center Robbie Tobeck said. "It really, really hurts."

The Hawks outgained Pittsburgh by 57 yards. They held the ball six minutes longer. They had six more first downs.

Matt Hasselbeck, the losing quarterback, played well. Ben Roethlisberger, the winning quarterback, was awful. It was the worst performance by a winning quarterback in the 40-year history of this game.

Roethlisberger was 9-for-21. His rating was 22.6. He threw two interceptions. But the Steelers are the World Champions. The Steelers made three plays. That's all. But that was enough.

"You can talk about Xs and Os, this and that, story lines. All of that's well and good in the week leading up to it," Tobeck said. "But on game day, it's who makes the most plays. We were prepared for what they showed us. But, you know, execution."

The Steelers' defense bent. The Seahawks' offense broke.

The Steelers couldn't cover Jerramy Stevens, but he covered himself. He dropped three passes. If he had caught all three, the Seahawks would have won. Pittsburgh's Hines Ward was the game's MVP, but Stevens was as much of a factor in the Steelers' win ➤

Ben Roethlisberger dives for the end zone at the end of the first half. The Pittsburgh quarterback fell on the goal line for a touchdown. Seattle challenged the play; it was reviewed and upheld.

7

Grant Wistrom, Seattle defensive end, celebrates his tackle of Roethlisberger behind the line of scrimmage in the second quarter, the only Seahawks sack of the Pittsburgh quarterback in the game.

➤ as Ward.

It was the Seahawks' game to win. And they lost it. This was their chance to take a championship back to Seattle. And they dropped it.

Shoulda. Woulda. Coulda.

Guard Chris Gray was flagged for a drive-stalling hold on one possession. Wide receiver Darrell Jackson and tackle Sean Locklear were victimized by bad penalty calls that cost the Seahawks two touchdowns.

Josh Brown missed long, but makeable field goals from 50 and 54 yards. Jackson didn't recognize a blitz leading to an incompletion late in the first half. Peter Warrick failed to catch a punt and allowed the ball to roll dead on the 2-yard line. And Hasselbeck threw a fourth-quarter interception at the Steelers' 27, after the Hawks had driven 71 yards.

"I can't really say much," offensive coordinator Gil Haskell said. "What can you say?"

This is the kind of loss that will gnaw at the Seahawks through the winter and through their off-season workouts. It will haunt their dreams.

The players will wake up out of a sound sleep in a cold sweat and remember the dropped passes, the missed field goals, the penalties, the punt that rolled dead on their 2-yard line.

They will look at the game film and realize they should have been ahead about 24-0 at halftime.

They will see that they kicked the Pittsburgh Steelers up and down Ford Field.

They will see Walter Jones burying Joey Porter deep into the artificial surface.

They will see Stevens running open in the middle of the field, time after time after time. ➤

Jerramy Stevens can't hang onto this pass in the second quarter. The incomplete pass on third-and-two ended a Seahawks drive at the Pittsburgh 47. Stevens dropped three passes in the game.

➤ But they will also see the blizzard of mistakes, and they will wince at what might have been.

"We stubbed our foot a couple of times," wide receiver Joe Jurevicius said. "And that's all I have to say on that."

A loss like this leaves you speechless. It makes you grope for answers that don't exist. It can make you look at your perfect game plan and wonder how it could have unraveled so badly.

"When it comes down to it, they threw the ball and ran the ball on three plays better than we did," Tobeck said.

Three plays were enough to win a Super Bowl.

Roethlisberger scrambling, then throwing across his body, across the field, to Ward on a third-and-28. Willie Parker breaking loose, one time and only one time, for 75 yards, the longest run in Super Bowl history. And Antwaan Randle El throwing a perfect reverse pass to Ward for a 43-yard touchdown.

"I felt the whole game we were going to win the game," Tobeck said. "I felt we were moving the ball on them, but it was a little frustrating not being able to finish the drives."

The Seahawks made the kind of mistakes you can't make in a Super Bowl. They didn't handle the enormity of the event. They beat up the Steelers, but they couldn't beat them. In their biggest game, they played their worst game.

"I'm more disappointed in how we played in certain areas," coach Mike Holmgren said. "I think we were careless with the football and we had way too many penalties."

The Seahawks could have won it all. They were better than the Steelers. But the mistakes they made on Super Bowl Sunday will follow them all the way to next summer, all the way to Cheney where the long hard pull toward another February will begin anew. ■

Steelers Willie Parker leaps in for a touchdown after his 75-yard run in the third quarter, giving Pittsburgh a 14-3 lead. The run was the longest from scrimmage in Super Bowl history, breaking the record of 74 yards set by Raiders Marcus Allen in Super Bowl XVIII (1984).

Jerome Bettis barges over three Seahawks in the third quarter. Bettis had 43 yards on 14 carries. The 13-year NFL veteran announced his retirement after the game.

With their team trailing in the third quarter, Seahawks fans at Detroit's Ford Field look concerned.

Pittsburgh players gather around Roethlisberger after a reverse-pass play went for 43 yards and a touchdown with 8:56 left in the fourth quarter. It would be the final score in the 21-10 victory over the Seahawks.

14

Seattle defensive end Grant Wistrom sits dejected after the 21-10 Seahawks loss to Pittsburgh.

Steelers Deshea Townsend sacks Matt Hasselbeck with 6:28 left in the game, forcing a Seattle punt. Pittsburgh took four minutes off the clock before Seattle got the ball back with 1:51 left in the game and failed to score.

A Steelers fan consoles Lorin Sandretzky, one of the Seattle supporters who made the trip to Super Bowl XL in Detroit.

15

1ST QUARTER

SCORING

Seattle	3				3
Pittsburgh	0				0

SUMMARY

The Seahawks led 3-0 at the end of a first quarter that was almost completely devoid of offense except for the Seattle passing combination of Matt Hasselbeck to Darrell Jackson. Jackson tied a Super Bowl record for passes caught in the first quarter with five, good for 50 yards.

Each team punted after its first two possessions.

On Seattle's third possession, a 19-yard Hasselbeck-to-Jackson pass moved the Seahawks to the Steeler 28. After an 11-yard gain, Hasselbeck hit Jackson for an apparent touchdown. But Jackson was called for using his hand to push away Steelers safety Chris Hope, and the TD was nullified. Seattle settled for a 47-yard Josh Brown field goal to go ahead 3-0.

The Steelers went three-and-out on all three of their possessions.

KEY PLAY

Seattle's Matt Hasselbeck dropped back, scrambled left and found Darrell Jackson (82) in the end zone on a 16-yard pass play. But Jackson was flagged for offensive pass interference, with officials ruling that he pushed off Steelers safety Chris Hope (28). The touchdown was nullified, and the Seahawks eventually settled for a field goal.

TEAM STATS

TIME OF POSSESSION

Steelers 4:30
Seahawks 10:30

RUSHING YARDS
19
15

PASSING YARDS
61
1

TOTAL NET YARDS
80
17

2ND QUARTER

SCORING

Seattle	3	0			3
Pittsburgh	0	7			7

SUMMARY

After going without a first down in the first quarter, the Steelers began to take control. The quarter began with a promising Seattle drive that ended when Jerramy Stevens dropped a pass at about the 30.

Pittsburgh reached its 48 before a Michael Boulware interception stopped the drive. Seattle went three-and-out, and Pittsburgh then moved into Seattle territory for the first time. A 37-yard pass from Ben Roethlisberger to Hines Ward on third-and-28 put the ball at the Seahawk 3. Roethlisberger then scored on third-and-goal from the 1, with the ball barely crossing the goal line. The play was reviewed, but the call stood, and Pittsburgh led 7-3.

Seattle then moved to the Pittsburgh 36-yard line, but a 54-yard field goal by Josh Brown sailed wide right.

KEY PLAYS

Facing third-and-28 at the Seattle 40, Steelers QB Ben Roethlisberger bought time by rolling to his left, then stopped and threw back to his right to receiver Hines Ward, who maneuvered behind Seahawk safety Michael Boulware. The play gained 37 yards and put the ball at the Seattle 3, setting up Pittsburgh's first touchdown.

TEAM STATS

TIME OF POSSESSION

Steelers 8:42
Seahawks 6:18

RUSHING YARDS
21
27

PASSING YARDS
53
69

TOTAL NET YARDS
74
96

3RD QUARTER

SCORING

Seattle	3	0	7		10
Pittsburgh	0	7	7		14

SUMMARY

The quarter featured two Super Bowl records: the longest run from scrimmage (75 yards for a touchdown by Pittsburgh's Willie Parker) and the longest interception return (76 yards by Seahawks Kelly Herndon). Parker's run came on the second play of the quarter and gave Pittsburgh a 14-3 lead.

After Seattle kicker Josh Brown missed a 50-yard field goal, Pittsburgh drove to the Seattle 7. On a third-down play, a Ben Roethlisberger pass was intercepted by Herndon and returned to the Steelers 20. On third down, Hasselbeck hit Jerramy Stevens for a 16-yard touchdown pass to make it 14-10. The quarter ended with the Seahawks moving on a drive that began at their 2-yard line.

KEY PLAYS

The 75-yard touchdown run by Steelers Willie Parker to put them ahead 14-3.

After that the Steelers seemed primed to put away the game. But facing third-and-six at Seattle's 7, Ben Roethlisberger underthrew Cedric Wilson, and Seattle's Kelly Herndon picked off the pass and returned it 76 yards to the Steelers' 20. Seattle scored three plays later to cut Pittsburgh's lead to 14-10.

TEAM STATS

TIME OF POSSESSION

Steelers 7:31
Seahawks 7:29

RUSHING YARDS
50
113

PASSING YARDS
68
31

TOTAL NET YARDS
118
144

4TH QUARTER

SCORING

Seattle	3	0	7	0	10
Pittsburgh	0	7	7	7	21

SUMMARY

The Seahawks were driving with a chance to take the lead as the quarter began, but a holding penalty on Sean Locklear nullified a pass completion to the 1-yard line. Two plays later, Matt Hasselbeck's pass to Darrell Jackson was intercepted by Ike Taylor, who returned it 24 yards to the Pittsburgh 29. The Steelers scored when receiver Antwaan Randle El took a reverse and threw a 43-yard touchdown to Hines Ward to make it 21-10 with 8:56 left. Seattle was forced to punt on its next possession. The Steelers took over with 6:15 left and went on a time-consuming drive that chewed up all but the final two minutes. Seattle's last-ditch drive ended on downs with three seconds left at the Pittsburgh 23 yard-line.

KEY PLAYS

Steelers' Antwaan Randle El passed 43 yards to Hines Ward to go ahead 21-10 with 8:56 left in the game. On the play, Ben Roethlisberger pitched to Willie Parker, who handed off to Randle El, a quarterback in college at Indiana. Ward, who lined up left, broke open running across the field and caught the pass in stride inside the 5-yard line and ran into the end zone.

TEAM STATS

TIME OF POSSESSION

Steelers 6:17
Seahawks 8:43

RUSHING YARDS
47
25

PASSING YARDS
77
57

TOTAL NET YARDS
124
82

Fireworks explode above Qwest Field before the Seahawks beat the Carolina Panthers, 34-14, to win the NFC Championship.

Seahawks never trail
as they roll past Carolina...

NFC Champs

...and earn their first trip
to the Super Bowl

17

SEAHAWKS
34
CAROLINA
14

HAWK HIGHLIGHTS

QB Matt Hasselbeck:
20-28, 219 yards, 2 TDs

RB Shaun Alexander:
34 carries, 132 yards, 2 TDs

DT Rocky Bernard:
2 sacks, helped front four
pressure Carolina QB Jake
Delhomme all game.

LB Lofa Tatupu:
Interception set up field
goal. Tatupu's head-on
collision with Carolina RB
Nick Goings knocked Goings
out of the game.

BY THE NUMBERS

33—Receiving yards by
Carolina's Steve Smith.
62—Yards allowed by
Seattle defense in first half.

EXTRA POINTS

No. 2 QB Seneca Wallace saw
time at receiver. His 28-yard
reception to the Carolina 17-
yard line set up Jerramy
Stevens touchdown catch on
the next play.

Super

Realization of a dream: Seahawks storm their way to the Super Bowl

BY STEVE KELLEY
Seattle Times staff columnist

Bowl

As confetti fell around him and fireworks exploded overhead, Seahawks safety Marquand Manuel knelt in disbelief, in the eye of the maelstrom at Qwest Field, tears rolling down his cheeks, overcome by the moment.

"Nobody deserves this more than you, nobody," teammate Bobby Engram said, wrapping an arm around Manuel's shoulder pads, consoling and celebrating at the same time.

"I just had to stop and pause for that moment to realize where I came from and what it took to get to this moment," Manuel said. "It all just hit me at one time.

"To come here from where I came from, from getting released to getting my first interception in a big-time game today. I couldn't write a better script. You wonder sometimes if hard work is going to pay off. Now I know that it does." ➤

Bound

Matt Hasselbeck holds up the George Halas trophy, given to the winner of the NFC Championship, while Shaun Alexander looks on at left.

Seattle's Marquand Manuel returns an interception to the 17-yard line in the first quarter, setting up the first of two Shaun Alexander touchdowns.

Fan Shane Goode raises a sign pointing the way to the Super Bowl in Detroit on Feb. 5, 2006.

➤ Left on the NFL's scrap heap after Cincinnati cut him in 2004, Manuel had fought his way onto the league's main stage. Maybe no player symbolizes this team, this city, this franchise, more than Seahawks free safety Manuel, an underdog in a city of underdogs.

In the din and the darkness, in the most important game in franchise history, in front of the whole football world, the Seahawks pitched as perfect a 60 minutes of football as this city has ever seen.

They didn't just beat the Carolina Panthers in Sunday's NFC Championship Game. They crushed them from kickoff to confetti. Beat them 34-14.

They completed a trip that was 30 years in the taking. The Seahawks are going to the Super Bowl. Pause and let that sink in. ➤

Defensive backs Jordan Babineaux and Marcus Trufant tackle Panthers receiver Steve Smith after he gains 4 yards in the second quarter. Smith was held to 33 yards on five catches.

➤ "You can sense this is a big deal to a lot of people," quarterback Matt Hasselbeck said.

The Seahawks, the franchise that has broken your heart more times than you care to remember; the franchise that had become the definition of .500 — Team Medi-hawk-rity — is going to Motown, going to Super Bowl XL.

"I've been through a lot of years that were very challenging," said fullback Mack Strong, a Seahawk since 1993. "A lot of turning points. But I can tell you in all honesty, with all my heart, this feeling that I have right now, getting ready to go to Detroit to play for the world championship, it's been worth every second.

"If you had told me when I first came into the league that it would take 12 years, but it would happen, I wouldn't have believed it. But if you had told me that's what it would take, if I could just hang on, I'd be like, 'Sure, I'll pay the price. I'll do whatever I got to do just to hang on that long.' "

First owner Paul Allen, then coach Mike Holmgren and finally Hasselbeck stood on the podium amid the smoke and joy and raised the NFC championship trophy above their heads. Center Robbie Tobeck watched, promising he wouldn't cry.

"I almost cried with about five minutes left in the game, but I'm not going to cry right now," Tobeck said. "I've got cold chills. All the hard work, all the ups and downs we've had the last six years, every bit of it has been worth it. Every ➤

Jerramy Stevens scores a touchdown in the first quarter on a 17-yard pass from Matt Hasselbeck.

23

Shaun Alexander gathers with the offensive line as they prepare to start the second quarter.

Fan Maureen Greene is decked out in Seahawk colors and earrings.

Shaun Alexander gets to the 1-yard line at the end of the first quarter.

Rocky Bernard gives his signature "Sugar Bear Shake" after sacking Carolina quarterback Jake Delhomme in the second quarter.

A flawless Hasselbeck announced his brilliance, throwing for 219 yards and two touchdowns. Shaun Alexander shook off the silly notion that he couldn't come up big in a game this large, rushing for more yards, 132, than he had in total in his three previous playoff games.

It was a rout.

Lofa Tatupu staggered Carolina with one interception. Manuel hit them with another one. And Michael Boulware stopped the last meaningful Carolina drive with another pick.

And as the clock ran down, the fans sang a chant so surreal, it almost didn't seem to fit with this city:

"Super Bowl. Super Bowl."

"We're here. We're doing it," Tobeck said "We're going to

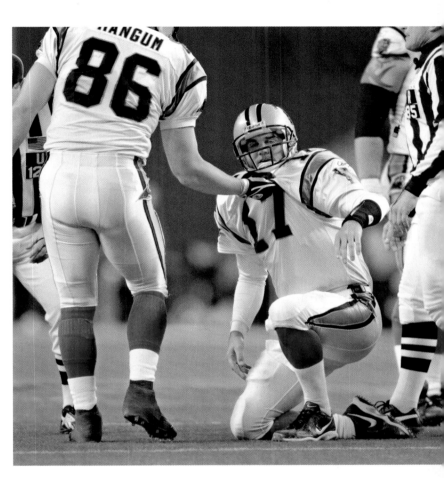

Panther quarterback Jake Delhomme is helped up by teammates after a sack by Rocky Bernard in the third quarter.

the Super Bowl, and I'm just as proud as I can be to be a member of the first Seahawks team to go to the Super Bowl."

Edgar Martinez's double in 1995 scored Ken Griffey Jr., and his teammates dogpiled on top of Griffey at home plate as the Kingdome shook after the Mariners beat the New York Yankees and won their first playoff series.

But this win was bigger.

Shawn Kemp outplayed Karl Malone in a Game 7 in the swelter of KeyArena, sending the Sonics to the NBA Finals in 1996.

This win was better.

Coach Lenny Wilkens and assistant Les Habegger ran off the floor hugging each other after the Sonics had won the ➤

27

Seahawks wide receiver Darrell Jackson does a bit of crowd surfing after a touchdown catch.

Matt Hasselbeck celebrates his first-quarter touchdown pass to Jerramy Stevens.

➤ NBA Finals in 1979 over the Washington Bullets.

That was a world championship. But this win felt more important, felt more meaningful than any win in the history of professional sports in this city.

"They've been die-hard sports fans in Seattle for a long time," defensive end Grant Wistrom said. "...It sure feels good to bring them what they've always wanted."

After 30 years, the Seahawks, the Seattle Seahawks are going to the Super Bowl.

Believe it. ■

29

Seahawks owner Paul Allen points to the fans in Qwest Field during the trophy presentation. He is flanked by Terry Bradshaw, left, emcee of the trophy presentation, and Mike McCormack, who once served as president and general manager for both the Seahawks and the Carolina Panthers.

Seahawks fans cheer as they drive through downtown Seattle after the team won the NFC Championship.

SCORING

Carolina	0	7	0	7	14
Seattle	10	10	7	7	34

1ST QUARTER

SEATTLE TOUCHDOWN—17-yard pass from Matt Hasselbeck to Jerramy Stevens. (Josh Brown extra point is good). 5:31 time remaining. (5 plays, 57 yards. Time of drive: 2:16). Key play: Hasselbeck 28-yard pass to Senaca Wallace to Panthers 17. **Seattle 7, Carolina 0**

SEATTLE FIELD GOAL—24-yarder by Brown. 2:23 time remaining. (6 plays, 14 yards. Time of drive: 2:44). Key plays: Lofa Tatupu 21-yard interception return to Panthers 20; Hasselbeck 11-yard pass to Stevens; Hasselbeck 5-yard run on 3rd-and-11. **Seattle 10, Carolina 0**

2ND QUARTER

SEATTLE TOUCHDOWN—1-yard run by Shaun Alexander. (Brown extra point is good). 14:53 time remaining. (4 plays, 17 yards. Time of drive: 0:57). Key plays: Marquand Manuel 32-yard interception return to Panthers 17; Alexander 15-yard run. **Seattle 17, Carolina 0**

CAROLINA TOUCHDOWN—59-yard punt return by Steve Smith. (John Kasay extra point is good). 9:05 time remaining. **Seattle 17, Carolina 7**

SEATTLE FIELD GOAL—39-yarder by Brown. 4:03 time remaining. (10 plays, 57 yards. Time of drive: 5:02). Key plays: Hasselbeck 17-yard pass to Darrell Jackson to Seahawks 39; Hasselbeck 4-yard run on 3rd-and-3; Alexander 11-yard and 18-yard runs; Hasselbeck 17-yard pass to Jackson on 3rd-and-27. **Seattle 20, Carolina 7**

3RD QUARTER

SEATTLE TOUCHDOWN—20-yard pass from Hasselbeck to Jackson. (Brown extra point is good). 11:09 time remaining. (8 plays, 65 yards. Time of drive: 3:51). Key plays: Josh Scobey 32-yard kickoff return; Alexander 16-yard run to Panthers 20. **Seattle 27, Carolina 7**

4TH QUARTER

SEATTLE TOUCHDOWN—1-yard run by Alexander. (Brown extra point is good). 6:00 time remaining. (8 plays, 53 yards. Time of drive: 4:48). Key plays: Hasselbeck 12-yard pass to Stevens; Hasselbeck 7-yard pass to Ryan Hannam. **Seattle 34, Carolina 7**

CAROLINA TOUCHDOWN—47-yard pass from Jake Delhomme to Drew Carter. (Kasay extra point is good). 5:09 time remaining. (4 plays, 80 yards. Time of Drive: 0:51). **Seattle 34, Carolina 14**

Attendance: 67,837

Seahawks fans turned out in full regalia for the NFC Championship Game.

> ❝ I've been through a lot of years that were very challenging. A lot of turning points. But I can tell you in all honesty, with all my heart, this feeling that I have right now, getting ready to go to Detroit to play for the world championship, it's been worth every second.❞
>
> — FULLBACK MACK STRONG, A SEAHAWK SINCE 1993

31

Seahawks end playoff drought

Seahawks win their first post-season game in over 20 years despite losing Shaun Alexander and three fumbles

BY JOSÉ MIGUEL ROMERO
Seattle Times staff writer

They wiped their brows and exhaled. Then they celebrated — players, coaches, the owner, fans and anyone else pulling for the Seahawks. That sound heard coming from Qwest Field as the game clock showed zeroes was as much a sigh of relief as it was a collective primal scream of joy. The city of Seattle and Seahawks Nation had waited more than two decades for a playoff victory, and finally it was theirs. ➤

"Get Loud" is the advice on one of the signs held up by a Seahawks fan in the second half of the playoff game against the Washington Redskins.

Matt Hasselbeck thrusts his fist in the air after completing a 37- yard pass to Darrell Jackson in the third quarter.

33

SEAHAWKS
20
REDSKINS
10

> ❝ This is a year of destiny, and we knew if we came out here and played together as a football team, we would find a way to win.❞ — FULLBACK MACK STRONG

Seahawks free safety Ken Hamlin shakes hands with fans before the NFC divisional game. Hamlin, whose season ended after he was injured in a fight outside a Seattle night club Oct. 17, raised the 12th Man flag.

Soaking it in

➤ That was all that mattered. The Seahawks made enough plays to win a rain-drenched NFC divisional playoff against the Washington Redskins, 20-10.

"I just feel like we're a team of destiny," fullback Mack Strong said. "This is a year of destiny, and we knew if we came out here and played together as a football team, we would find a way to win."

The Seahawks made enough mistakes to lose, with three lost fumbles, two on special teams in their own territory. And that wasn't all they had to overcome to win and break the NFL's longest post-season victory drought.

Running back Shaun Alexander was lost for the game when, with 4:29 left in the first quarter, he suffered a concussion upon impact with two Washington defenders and the turf following a run for a 1-yard loss.

Alexander struggled to get to his feet with help from trainers as the playoff-record crowd of 67,551 chanted "MVP! MVP!" in support of the NFL's Most Valuable Player and rushing champion.

He wobbled to the sideline and never came back into the game. Moments before, Alexander had fumbled at the Washington 11-yard line as the Seahawks were taking their opening drive down the field with authority.

It was just his second lost fumble of the season. Without him, the Seahawks' offense sputtered for a time.

After the game, coach Mike Holmgren indicated that Alexander's concussion was not of high grade but that he will be administered tests. He would be there for the Seahawks the next week ➤

SCORING

Washington	0	3	0	7	**10**
Seattle	0	7	7	6	**20**

HAWK HIGHLIGHTS

QB Matt Hasselbeck:
16-26, 215 yards, TD
21 yards rushing, TD

WR Darrell Jackson:
9 catches, 143 yards, TD

Defensive ends Grant Wistrom and Bryce Fisher:
Combined for 12 tackles and kept Washington QB Mark Brunell on the run all game.

PLAY OF THE GAME

Hasselbeck threw a 29-yard touchdown pass to Jackson, putting the Seahawks ahead to stay, 7-3.

EXTRA POINTS

RB Maurice Morris came in after Shawn Alexander was hurt in the first quarter and went 49 yards on 18 carries. He ran for 3 first downs in Seattle's first touchdown drive.

Washington quarterback Mark Brunell faces the Seahawks defense on the field and the face of a screaming fan on the screen at Qwest Field.

Seahawks Jimmy Williams fumbles a punt in the second quarter, leading to a Washington field goal...

...and Josh Scobey fumbles a kickoff in the fourth quarter, but this time Washington missed the field goal.

35

➤ against Carolina, Holmgren said.

And there will be a next week, thanks in large part to quarterback Matt Hasselbeck, wide receiver Darrell Jackson, ball carriers Strong and Maurice Morris and a defense that knuckled up and answered the call when momentum shifted to the visitors from the nation's capital.

Hasselbeck connected with Jackson for a 29-yard touchdown pass in the second quarter to give the Seahawks the lead. That came after punt returner Jimmy Williams' fumble led to a Washington field goal.

Hasselbeck also ran for a touchdown, his 6-yard sprint to the right corner of the end zone giving the Seahawks a 14-3 lead and capping an 81-yard drive in the third quarter.

Jackson was all heart after returning from a back injury that forced him out of the game briefly. He caught nine passes for a team-playoff-record 143 yards.

Morris, who filled in for Alexander, rushed for 49 ➤

Darrell Jackson watches the ball come into his hands for a reception in the first quarter. Jackson caught a touchdown pass later in the game.

Seattle linebacker Lofa Tatupu takes down Mark Brunell after a 2-yard gain on third-and-five in the first quarter. Tatupu had 10 tackles in the game.

Shaun Alexander is helped off the field after suffering a concussion in the first quarter. He did not play in the rest of the game.

Seahawks fullback Mack Strong, who picked up much of the load for the injured Alexander, gains 32 yards on a third-and-six play in the fourth quarter, the longest run in Strong's 13-year career.

Taylor Jacobs of the Redskins is stopped by Seahawks Andre Dyson, Bryce Fisher, left, and Marquand Manuel (33) early in the second quarter, ending a Washington drive.

> **"** It sure doesn't seem like it should have taken this long to win another (playoff game). I'm glad they got that skunk out of the way."

— FORMER SEAHAWKS WIDE RECEIVER STEVE LARGENT

Matt Hasselbeck shows the ball to Seahawks fans after scoring a 6-yard touchdown...

➤ yards and picked up two important first downs on third-and-ones during Seattle's first scoring drive. Strong sealed the victory with a 32-yard run with less than five minutes to play in the game and the Seahawks needing to make a third-and-six to keep the clock running.

All the while, the Seahawks' defense was doing its part to keep Washington from scoring. It allowed just 59 rushing yards and spent practically the entire afternoon in the backfield in dogged pursuit of Washington quarterback Mark Brunell.

"The teams that really believe in each other understand the game is not over," defensive Chuck Darby said of the team's response to the loss of Alexander and the team's turnovers. "If your brother went out there and fumbled the ball, go out there and get the ball back for him. Let him know we're going to get the ball back. That's how you win games. If you feel sorry for yourself, it's over."

As Darby spoke, team president Tim Ruskell walked over to his locker with CEO Tod Leiweke and congratulated Darby.

"You were a warrior today," Ruskell said. "As always."

Darby wasn't alone, and that's why the Seahawks are still alive. ∎

... and then gives it to Jeremy Yousef, who celebrates with David Tall, left, and Mike Gabelein in the stands at Qwest Field.

42

Fireworks and victory flags after Seattle's 20-10 win over Washington.

43

The long runs.
The touchdowns.
The celebration routines.
The smile. The laugh.
The records. Seahawks running back Shaun Alexander will be remembered for all that, and one other thing: winning the NFL Most Valuable Player award.

MVP

BY JOSÉ MIGUEL ROMERO
Seattle Times staff writer

Alexander led the NFL in rushing in the 2005 season, and set a league season record with 28 touchdowns. He received 19 of 50 votes from a nationwide panel of media covering the NFL.

Alexander credited his coaches and teammates.

"We just feel it's exciting," Alexander said. "All the guys, they all say it just like I want them to say it, that *we* won the MVP. And we have."

Alexander, 28, is the first Seahawk to be named MVP, an award that began in 1957 when Cleveland running back Jim Brown ➤

Shaun Alexander ran through the Houston defense for 141 yards and 4 touchdowns.

➤ won it. Before Alexander, the last running back to win it was Marshall Faulk of the St. Louis Rams, who won it in 2000, the year he scored a record 26 touchdowns.

That record has since been broken twice, Alexander doing it this year.

Alexander gained 1,880 yards to win his first NFL rushing title. He led the league in points scored with 168. He was named NFC offensive player of the week three times and offensive player of the month for November. On Oct. 23 in the game against Dallas, he passed Chris Warren to become the Seahawks' all-time leading rusher and has 7,817 yards in his six-year career.

His 88-yard run at Arizona on Nov. 6 tied his record for the longest run from scrimmage in team history.

Other milestones in 2005: Alexander became one of only four NFL players to score 20 or more touchdowns in back-to-back seasons. He had two games with four touchdowns in each, and became just the second NFL player to accomplish that in a season.

Alexander became the first NFL player to score 15 or more touchdowns in five straight seasons when he scored three against St. Louis on Nov. 13 at Qwest Field. He is the 16th player in league history to rush for 1,800 or more yards in a season. He gained 100 yards or more in 11 games this season.

"Let's just say Shaun put us on the map up here," fullback Mack Strong said. "The secret's out about the type of team we have out here and the type of players we have out here. You look at his stats and what they mean to the team, and I think they have a lot to do with where we're at.

"Everyone on this team is super excited for Shaun."

Many teams didn't respect Alexander and had the idea that he wasn't a tough runner before they faced him. By the end of the game, however, defenders were saying Alexander was better than they thought.

The question that remains is whether the Seahawks will sign Alexander to a long-term contract.

Alexander played this season with a one-year, $6.32 million deal, with the ability to become a free agent if he is not re-signed. The MVP would be quite a bargaining chip for Alexander in his agents' negotiations with the Seahawks, which were suspended by mutual agreement until the end of the season.

Seahawks coach Mike Holmgren expressed his happiness for Alexander.

"I'm as tough on him as anyone I've ever coached," Holmgren said. "He listened, and he tried. That makes me feel good, because he's gotten better."

Alexander had his own perspective on the MVP award.

"I never really thought about whether it could be done or not, because awards are exciting but they're not the end-all, be-all," Alexander said. "Being 13-3 was a goal for us… Those all come with setting the first goal, which is being good." ∎

Shaun Alexander waves to the crowd after the 42-10 Seahawks win over the Houston Texans.

SHAUN ALEXANDER

- 2005 NFL MVP
- NFL OFFENSIVE PLAYER OF THE YEAR
- 1ST TEAM ALL-PRO
- PRO BOWL PLAYER
- NFL SINGLE-SEASON TOUCHDOWN RECORD

Height: 5-11
Weight: 225
Born: Aug. 8, 1977
Hometown: Florence, Ky.

High-school career: Parade and USA Today All American at Boone County High School. Gatorade Circle of Champions Kentucky Player of the Year. Ranks fifth on prep national career-record list with 110 touchdowns.

College: University of Alabama's all-time rushing leader with 3,565 yards in four seasons. Graduated with a degree in marketing in 1999 and left holding 15 Crimson Tide records and three Southeastern Conference ones. Academic All-SEC as senior.

Drafted as pro: Seattle had 19th pick in first round of the 2000 NFL draft and took Alexander.

Pro Bowl: Selection to Pro Bowl team is his third. Named to the All-Pro first team for 2005, second team in 2004.

Personal: He and his wife Valerie have two daughters. He says he would like to have four sons as well.

Battling the heat in Cheney, defensive lineman Antonio Cochran blows a spray of water during a break. By the end of camp, though, Cochran was gone, failing to make the cut.

New cornerback Kelly Herndon (31) works against receivers during a seven-on-seven drill.

July, August bring heat – and high expectations

The Seattle Seahawks started the training camp for their 30th year with high expectations, plenty of new names and faces and one big difference: Walter Jones, all 315 pounds of him.

It was his first appearance at Seahawks training camp in four years, after three straight summers of missing camp in hopes of getting the long-term contract deal he sought.

This year, he signed a seven-year, $52.5 million contract in February and showed up at Eastern Washington University in Cheney to run sprints in the 94-degree heat with the team.

"There's nothing I missed about Cheney," Jones said, "but it's still great to be back with the guys."

One of the guys not there was running back Shaun Alexander, whose wife Valerie was having their second child. He arrived a few days after his daughter's birth.

Offensive linemen Chris Gray and Walter Jones run sprints during a workout in 90-degree temperatures. Jones was in camp for the first time in four years.

JAGUARS
26
SEAHAWKS
14

GAME 1
AT JACKSONVILLE

Winning season had humble start

The Seahawks stumbled and fumbled away their opener in withering Florida heat

Talk about an inauspicious start. In their first regular-season game, the Seahawks committed five turnovers, lacked offensive punch and mostly let the Jacksonville Jaguars have their way with quarterback Matt Hasselbeck, who threw two interceptions and fumbled twice. Two of those turnovers led to the Jaguars scoring in Jacksonville's 26-14 victory at Alltel Stadium.

The five turnovers were the most since the 2000 season opener in Miami when the Seahawks had six.

It was bad from the beginning as Josh Scobey lost the ball on the game's opening kickoff return, resulting in a field goal for Jacksonville.

The Seahawks went ahead 7-6 on the first play of the second quarter, a 33-yard Hasselbeck touchdown pass to Joe Jurevicius. Their final lead came with 47 seconds left in the first half. Hasselbeck hit Darrell Jackson from 9 yards away, with Jackson edging over the goal line to make the score 14-13.

But on Jacksonville's first possession of the second half, they drove 78 yards and took the lead for good when quarterback Byron Leftwich hit wide receiver Jimmy Smith for a 7-yard touchdown. Smith, running along the sideline with Seahawks cornerback Marcus Trufant in his face, made the play of the game, tipping the ball to himself for the catch.

After that, the Seahawks didn't

Seahawk quarterback Matt Hasselbeck wipes sweat away late in the game. He threw two interceptions and fumbled twice.

move the ball into Jaguars territory until their final drive. The result? Hasselbeck fumbled and Jaguars ➤

SCORING

Seattle	0	14	0	0	14
Jacksonville	6	7	7	6	26

HAWK HIGHLIGHTS

RB Shaun Alexander:
14 carries, 73 yards

QB Matt Hasselbeck:
21-37, 246 yards,
2 interceptions, 2 fumbles

WR Bobby Engram
8 catches, 79 yards

WR Darrell Jackson:
6 catches, 65 yards, 1 TD

WR Joe Jurevicius
3 catches, 64 yards, 1 TD

BY THE NUMBERS

5 — Seahawks turnovers
0 — Jacksonville turnovers

EXTRA POINTS

Defensive tackle Rocky Bernard came off the bench to make two tackles, a seven-yard sack and a two-yard stop in the Jacksonville backfield.

Jacksonville's Jimmy Smith makes a one-handed grab over Seattle cornerback Marcus Trufant for the third quarter touchdown that put the Jaguars in the lead for good.

"

Jacksonville did what they wanted to do against us, which is throw us around. They totally controlled the whole game."

— RUNNING BACK SHAUN ALEXANDER

Seattle quarterback Matt Hasselbeck fumbles as he is hit by Jacksonville linebacker Akin Ayodele in the fourth quarter.

Seattle coach Mike Holmgren talks with defensive end Grant Wistrom, who had four tackles, deflected two passes and pressured Jacksonville quarterback Byron Leftwich into three bad throws.

Seattle running back Shaun Alexander tries unsuccessfully to convince field judge Tom Sifferman that a catch by Darrell Jackson was inbounds.

➤ defensive end Paul Spicer recovered the ball with two seconds left.

Smith burned the Seahawks' secondary with seven catches for 130 yards and two touchdowns.

The weather also could be described as burning, with the thermometer at kickoff showing 82 degrees and the field temperature hitting 120 degrees at one point. The Seahawks were dressed in their dark blue jerseys instead of the normal road whites because the Jaguars wanted to wear white. But Seattle refused to offer that as an excuse.

"Jacksonville did what they wanted to do against us, which is throw us around," running back Shaun Alexander said. "They totally controlled the whole game." ■

SEAHAWKS

21

FALCONS

18

SCORING

Atlanta	0	0	10	8	18
Seattle	0	21	0	0	21

HAWK HIGHLIGHTS

RB Shaun Alexander:
28 carries, 144 yards, 1 TD

QB Matt Hasselbeck:
20-31, 281 yards, 2 TD

WR Darrell Jackson:
8 catches, 131 yards

LB Lofa Tatupu:
6 tackles, 1 sack

BY THE NUMBERS

428—Seahawks total yards
223—Atlanta total yards

EXTRA POINTS

TE Jerramy Stevens made a diving catch for a 35-yard touchdown, giving the Seahawks a 21-0 lead at halftime.

The Seahawks held Falcons quarterback Michael Vick to 123 yards passing and 43 yards rushing.

Ⓛ Ⓦ ⬤ ⬤ ⬤ ⬤ ⬤ ⬤ ⬤ ⬤ ⬤ ⬤ ⬤ ⬤ ⬤ ⬤

Seahawks hang on for season's first win

Defensive backs swat away signs of team's past disasters

During the Seahawks' home opener, this thought went through coach Mike Holmgren's mind: "Oh my goodness, here we go again."

Again would be going down to defeat in the last part of a game after dominating for most of it — something that happened twice in the 2004 season, against the St. Louis Rams and the Dallas Cowboys.

But this time, the Seahawks didn't collapse. They made the plays they needed to make when they needed to make them and jogged off as 21-18 winners over the Atlanta Falcons before 66,030 fans at Qwest Field.

As Holmgren said, "It worked out for us at the end."

That's when Seahawks free safety Ken Hamlin and cornerback Andre Dyson swatted away quarterback Matt Schaub's pass on fourth-and-14 from the Atlanta 23 with 1:41 left in the game, a last-ditch effort to keep alive a drive. The Seahawks took over on downs, and, after an 11-yard run by Shaun Alexander, took two kneeldowns and cemented their first win of the season.

Atlanta was down 21-0 at the end of the first half when Seattle outgained Atlanta 288 to 78 in total yards, picked up 17 first downs to the Falcons' three and forced Atlanta to punt five times on six possessions. Alexander ran for one touchdown and quarterback Matt Hasselbeck passed for two more, one to Jerramy Stevens and one to Joe Jurevicius. ➤

Shaun Alexander brushes past umpire Bill Schuster on his way to some of his 144 yards rushing against Atlanta

"" Those opportunities in the past, when we had them, we didn't make the plays when we needed to, and this time we did. That's the difference."

— SEAHAWKS FULLBACK MACK STRONG

The Seahawks take the field during pregame introductions for the season's home opener at Qwest Field.

Atlanta quarterback Michael Vick narrowly escapes being sacked by Rocky Bernard. The Seattle defense kept steady pressure on Vick, who eventually left the game with a sore hamstring.

➤ Then the Seahawks lost their edge, and the Falcons scored 18 unanswered points — a touchdown pass from Michael Vick to Brian Finneran, a 1-yard run by T.J. Duckett (plus two-point conversion) and a 30-yard Todd Peterson field goal.

But the Seahawks' relentless defensive pressure finally wore down Vick, who grabbed his left hamstring after a 32-yard run and eventually left the game for Schaub to finish.

"It's just a matter of guys just understanding it's time to make plays," Seahawks fullback Mack Strong said. "Those opportunities in the past, when we had them, we didn't make the plays when we needed to, and this time we did. That's the difference." ■

Seattle's Ken Hamlin (26) and Andre Dyson (21) nearly intercept a pass intended for Roddy White (84) on fourth down with 1:41 left in the game, ending Atlanta's drive and their chances at a comeback win.

SEAHAWKS

37

CARDINALS

12

Shaun Alexander is all smiles in the fourth quarter. He had 140 yards and four touchdowns.

Winning looks easy against the Cardinals

A special time, too, as Chuck Knox is honored

The Seahawks dominated in all phases of the game.

The defense forced its first two turnovers of the season. The offense scored its first second-half points of the season, 27 of them. Shaun Alexander tied former Seahawk Chris Warren for first place in number of career 100-yard rushing games with his 24th.

And in a nice change from the week before for the frazzled fans at Qwest Field, the Seahawks made winning look easy as they swept past the Arizona Cardinals, 37-12.

Alexander ripped off 140 yards on 22 carries and scored four touchdowns, including a 25-yard scoring run in the first half. Matt Hassellbeck completed 20 of 31 passes for 242 yards on his 30th birthday.

For the second week in a row, the Seahawks' defense ran a quarterback right off the field, pressuring Arizona's Kurt Warner so much that when he tried to scramble late in the first half, he hurt a groin muscle and had to leave the game.

Against the Seattle defense, the Cardinals had to settle for four Neil Rackers field goals. Seahawks kicker Josh Brown had three.

The winless Cardinals kept it close for a while, trailing 10-9 at halftime. But in the second half they got only one more field ➤

Defensive end Grant Wistrom pumps his arms in celebration after stopping Arizona's J.J. Arrington for a 2-yard loss.

SCORING

Arizona	3	6	3	0	12
Seattle	7	3	14	13	37

HAWK HIGHLIGHTS

RB Shaun Alexander:
22 carries, 140 yards, 4 TDs

QB Matt Hasselbeck:
20-31, 242 yards

WR Darrell Jackson:
8 catches, 125 yards

SS Michael Boulware:
5 tackles, sack, forced fumble

BY THE NUMBERS

29 — Seahawks first downs
15 — Arizona first downs
447 — Total yards for the Seahawks, the most in a game so far this season.

EXTRA POINTS

CB Jordan Babineaux had six tackles, an interception and broke up a pass play in his first action beyond special teams and special defensive packages..

Seattle wide receiver Darrell Jackson makes one of his eight catches as Antrel Rolle tries to knock away the ball. Jackson had 125 yards receiving.

Shaun Alexander celebrates after scoring a touchdown in the third quarter against Arizona.

Seahawks defensive end Bryce Fisher hits Arizona quarterback Kurt Warner after Warner releases a pass that falls incomplete in the second quarter. Warner later left the game with a groin injury

➤ goal, and the Seahawks got their 27 points: three touchdowns on 1-yard runs by Alexander, and two field goals and three extra points by Brown.

Alexander's last touchdown capped the third 80-yard scoring drive of the day for the Seahawks.

Could anything make it a more perfect day? How about it all happening when former Seahawks coach Chuck Knox was inducted into the Seahawks' Ring of Honor? Knox had an 80-63 record in the nine seasons (1983 to 1991) he coached the Seahawks, taking the team to its only playoff wins (three) before this year.

Knox told the 64,843 fans they were the best in the world and listened as Mike Holmgren, the current coach, expressed his admiration: "I always appreciated how he coached, his toughness, and I will always appreciate the time he spent with a young coach coming into this league." ■

Former Seahawks coach Chuck Knox acknowledges the cheering crowd at his induction to the Seahawks' Ring of Honor.

L W W L

REDSKINS
20
OVERTIME
17
SEAHAWKS

Seahawks kicker Josh Brown reacts after missing a 47-yard field goal that would have won the game.

Overtime loss a game of "if onlys"

Potential winning kick bounces off upright

The 20-17 overtime loss to Washington was a game of "if onlys" for the Seahawks.

If only kicker Josh Brown's 47-yard field-goal attempt had not hit the left upright and bounced away on the final play of regulation.

If only defensive end Bryce Fisher had gotten a firmer grip on quarterback Mark Brunell on third-and-nine from the Washington 37 in overtime. A sack or even a tackle in that spot, and Washington would have had to punt the ball to the Seahawks.

Instead, Washington gained another first down and got in position for Nick Novak's winning 39-yard field goal.

The Seahawks battled back from deficits of 14-3 and 17-10 in the second half to force overtime. The offense engineered drives of 85 and 91 yards in the second half, both ending in touchdowns. A 3-yard touchdown run by Shaun Alexander in the third quarter made it 14-10 before Washington added ➤

OH, SO CLOSE: Seattle lost despite outgaining Washington by 2 yards, 354-352

SCORING

					OT	
Seattle	3	0	7	7	0	17
Washington	0	7	10	0	3	20

HAWK HIGHLIGHTS

RB Shaun Alexander:
20 carries, 98 yards, TD

QB Matt Hasselbeck:
26-38, 242 yards, TD

WR Bobby Engram:
9 catches, 106 yards
in 3 quarters

MLB Lofa Tatupu:
10 tackles, sack

BY THE NUMBERS

1-3 — Seahawks FG-Attempts
2-3 — Washington
FG-Attempts

EXTRA POINTS

WR Bobby Engram cracked ribs on the Seahawks first offensive play but stayed in the game for three quarters.

Reserve DT Craig Terrill was the first Seahawk to block a field goal kick since 1999.

Washington kicker Nick Novak (3) celebrates after hitting a 39-yard field goal in overtime to beat Seattle.

During the fourth-quarter drive that ended with Seattle tying the score, Seattle's Matt Hasselbeck runs for a first down in a fourth-and-one situation.

Seahawks coach Mike Holmgren tries to get the attention of the officials during overtime.

Seattle cornerback Kelly Herndon looks for running room after intercepting a Mark Brunell pass with a minute left in the fourth quarter and the score tied at 17.

➤ another field goal.

The Seattle defense kept Washington off the scoreboard in the fourth quarter, and with 1:27 left, Matt Hasselbeck hit Darrell Jackson in the end zone. Brown's kick for the extra point tied the score.

Washington got the ball back, but with a minute left in regulation, Seattle cornerback Kelly Herndon intercepted a Brunell pass and was tackled at the Washington 33-yard line.

Alexander had two chances to shorten the distance for Brown but could only gain 4 yards. Still, Brown thought his kick was perfect.

"I think it's the best ball I've hit in my life," he said. "It went exactly where I wanted it to go. Unfortunately, the upright got right in the way."

Afterward, heads were hanging and voices were lowered in the Seattle locker room at FedEx Field.

"I told [the players] that if you don't feel bad, then something is wrong with you," coach Mike Holmgren said. "But… you don't have the luxury of feeling bad for too long."

Forget the loss quickly, Holmgren urged his players, it's only a week to the showdown with their arch-rival St. Louis Rams. ■

Washington's Mike Sellers stretches for the end zone and scores in the third quarter despite the attention of Seattle's D.D. Lewis. The TD and extra point gave Washington a 14-10 lead.

Seahawks fan Gavin DeCapua celebrates with Seattle's Darrell Jackson after Jackson scored the tying touchdown in the fourth quarter.

"

Knowing that 52 other guys battled it out for 60 minutes and I have one second and it didn't work... It's a pretty unfortunate feeling. It's pretty downing, but we have 12 games to go."

— SEAHAWKS KICKER JOSH BROWN

SEAHAWKS

37

RAMS

31

The Seattle Times

SPORTS

Baseball playoffs

Astros advance after epic 18

Solving St. Louis

FOR THE SON HE LOVED, JUREVICIUS PLAYS

getting a boost

Positive EPO results put marathoner's life on hold

SCORING

Seattle	14	10	10	3	37
St. Louis	7	14	7	3	31

HAWK HIGHLIGHTS

RB Shaun Alexander:
25 carries, 119 yards, 2 TD

QB Matt Hasselbeck:
27-38, 316 yards

WR Joe Jurevicius:
9 catches, 137 yards, TD

MLB Lofa Tatupu:
9 solo tackles, interception

BY THE NUMBERS

4—punts inside the 20 by Seahawks punter Tom Rouen
1—punt inside the 20 for Rams punters

EXTRA POINTS

J.P. Darche, Seahawks long snapper, hustled downfield and recovered the ball after Jordan Babineaux knocked it loose from the Rams Shaun McDonald. The Seahawks then ran out the clock.

Seattle rules the Rams on the road

St. Louis jinx is a thing of the past

Forget the past, the Seahawks said.

Seattle is a different team from the past three seasons, when visiting the Edward Jones Dome brought three losses at the hands of their NFC West rivals, the St. Louis Rams.

So what if the Seahawks had lost four in a row to the Rams? This was a new day.

"We expected to win," Seahawks quarterback Matt Hasselbeck said.

And win they did — 37-31 to take over first place in the NFC West.

That Seahawks confidence might have been shattered with the opening kickoff when Rams returner Chris Johnson went 99 yards untouched into the end zone.

But the Seahawks answered with two touchdowns of their own in the first quarter, a 1-yard run by Shaun Alexander and a 29-yard pass from Hasselbeck to tight end Jerramy Stevens.

St. Louis scored first in the second quarter, tying the score on a 25-yard touchdown pass from quarterback Marc Bulger to wide receiver Kevin Curtis.

Then Joe Jurevicius caught a pass and ran in for a Seattle touchdown. St. Louis added another touchdown before Josh Brown closed first-half scoring with a field goal, giving Seattle a 24-21 lead.

The Seahawks kept ahead of the Rams in the second half after two more field goals by Brown and Alexander's second touchdown run and led 37-28 with 7:37 left in the game. But the Rams pulled to six points down with 3:54 left after a Jeff Wilkins field goal.

Seattle couldn't move the ball and had to punt. That's when the Rams made the critical mistake of the game. Shaun McDonald caught the punt for the Rams but was stripped of the ball by Seattle cornerback Jordan Babineaux. J.P. Darche, Seattle's long snapper, fell on the fumble, and the Seahawks ran out the clock to put an end to past frustrations against the Rams.

Seattle had two new starters at wide receiver, Jurevicius and D.J. Hackett, playing for Bobby Engram, out with cracked ribs, and Darrell Jackson, who had arthroscopic knee surgery. Jurevicius responded with nine catches for 137 yards and a touchdown, and Hackett's five catches for 43 yards included his first reception in the NFL.

"We're a bunch of no-names going into a tough game, and I think we showed we can play tough football," Jurevicius said

Seattle defenders Marquand Manuel (33), Jordan Babineaux (27), Marcus Trufant (23) and Grant Wistrom (98) topple Rams running back Steven Jackson. The Seattle defense held Jackson to 77 yards and one touchdown.

Joe Jurevicius eludes a tackle by St. Louis' Chris Johnson. Jurevicius caught nine passes for 137 yards and a touchdown.

Seahawks quarterback Matt Hasselbeck (8) gets chippy with Rams defensive tackle Damione Lewis.

Seahawks long snapper J.P. Darche (52) is hugged by teammate Josh Brown after Darche recovered a fumbled punt to seal Seattle's victory in St. Louis.

SEAHAWKS
42

TEXANS
10

SCORING

Houston	0	3	7	0	10
Seattle	14	7	7	14	42

HAWK HIGHLIGHTS

RB Shaun Alexander:
22 carries, 141 yards, 4 TD

RB Maurice Morris:
8 carries, 104 yards, TD

QB Matt Hasselbeck:
14-20, 168 yards, TD

BY THE NUMBERS

64%—Seahawks third-down efficiency
38%—Texans third-down efficiency
158—Hasselbeck's consecutive pass attempts without an interception, which broke Jim Zorn's team record.

TURNING POINT

When the teams stepped on the field. Seattle stopped Houston on its first possession, drove in for a 7-0 lead and never looked back.

L W W L W W ● ● ● ● ● ● ● ● ● ●

Seahawks take Houston in stride

Seattle sets a team record with 320 yards rushing

The Seahawks literally ran away with this game, a 42-10 routing of the Houston Texans before 66,196 happy fans at Qwest Field and a Sunday-night audience on ESPN.

Seattle had two running backs rush for more than 100 yards in the game for only the third time in team history. Shaun Alexander had 141 yards rushing and four touchdowns. His backup, Maurice Morris, gained 104 yards on eight carries and had one touchdown.

Even Matt Hasselbeck, not known for his fleetness of foot, averaged 10 yards a carry.

The 320 total yards rushing set a team game record. That meant a lot to the offensive line, those clearing the way for the running backs.

"In this league really, it's hard to run the ball like that," left guard Steve Hutchinson said. "When you have a good running game, you end up with 120 yards in this league and you're happy."

Seattle also had a consistent game in the air with Hasselbeck completing passes to six different receivers for 168 yards. And that was without starting receivers Darrell Jackson and Bobby Engram, still out with injuries. The reception committee that took their place: Jerheme Urban (two catches for 37 yards), Jerramy Stevens (two

catches for 28 yards), Peter Warrick (three catches, 53 yards), Joe Jurevicius (three catches, 29 yards, one touchdown), Mack Strong (three catches, 20 yards) and Alexander (one catch, one yard).

On defense, the Seahawks held the winless Texans to 227 yards.

"All in all, this is how you envision yourself playing every week," Jurevicius said. "Sometimes it doesn't happen, but you should enjoy it when they do come along."

Shaun Alexander picks up some of the 141 yards he had against Houston. Alexander also ran for four touchdowns.

Jerheme Urban makes a first-down catch on the Seahawks' first touchdown drive. Urban finished with two receptions for 37 yards in the 42-10 victory.

Seahawks defenders crush Texans running back Domanick Davis in the first quarter. Davis was held to 40 yards.

Seahawks running back Maurice Morris gained 104 yards on eight carries and scored a touchdown.

"

They dictate the game. They make you have to stop them. Teams like that, they're going to end up going a long way"

— TEXANS CORNERBACK
DUNTA ROBINSON

SEAHAWKS

13

COWBOYS

10

L W W L W W W ○ ○ ○ ○ ○ ○ ○

> "
> **A win like this takes the question away of whether we can do it. We've done it now."**
> — CENTER ROBBIE TOBECK

Brown's field goal downs Cowboys

Kicker prepared for victory celebration

Josh Brown's kick was still on its way to becoming the time-expired, 50-yard field goal that would give the Seahawks a 13-10 victory over Dallas when he started planning for the ensuing celebration.

"The moment I hit it, I knew I was about to get bombarded by my teammates, so I took my helmet off," he said. "That way they couldn't throw me to the ground."

His instincts, just like his kick, were dead on. The Seahawks, who improved to 5-2, rushed the field to swarm Brown. Even team owner Paul Allen and team president Tim Ruskell joined the party, and probably most of the 67,046 fans at Qwest Field would have if they could.

Jordan Babineaux set up the kick when, with 14 seconds left in a 10-10 game and Dallas driving, he picked off a pass by Dallas quarterback Drew Bledsoe and returned it 25 yards before stepping out of bounds at the ➤

Seattle wide receiver Jerheme Urban leaps high over Dallas cornerback Anthony Henry to make a 22-yard reception at the start of Seattle's fourth-quarter touchdown drive.

SCORING

Dallas	7	0	0	3	10
Seattle	0	3	0	10	13

HAWK HIGHLIGHTS

DE Bryce Fisher:
9 tackles, 2 sacks

QB Matt Hasselbeck:
23-42, 224 yards, TD, 2 IN

RB Shaun Alexander:
21 carries, 61 yards

BY THE NUMBERS

2-2 Seahawks FG-attempts
1-2 Dallas FG-attemps

EXTRA POINTS

Shaun Alexander ran for only 61 yards but it was enough to set a team record for career rushing yards — 6,713.

Measurable rain fell at Qwest Field for the first time during a Seahawks game since the stadium opened in 2002. The wet conditions seemed to contribute to 6 fumbles and 4 interceptions.

Josh Brown, sans helmet, celebrates as he leaves the field after his winning field goal.

➤ Cowboys' 32-yard line, leaving five seconds for Brown.

Brown had drilled a 55-yard field goal with 33 seconds left in the first half for the Seahawks' first points. Safety Michael Boulware set up those points when he intercepted a Bledsoe pass and returned it 31 yards.

Dallas led 7-3 at halftime on a 5-yard, first-quarter touchdown pass from Bledsoe to Keyshawn Johnson. The Cowboys didn't score again until late

Seahawks safety Marquand Manuel holds up Ken Hamlin's jersey to the Qwest Field crowd before the game. Hamlin, a Seattle free safety, did not play after being injured in a fight outside a Seattle nightclub earlier in the week.

in the fourth quarter after Roy Williams picked off a pass by Seahawks quarterback Matt Hasselbeck at the Seattle 24-yard line. Dallas kicked a field goal for a 10-3 lead with 2:01 left.

That's when the game's heroes emerged. Wide receiver Jerheme Urban made a leaping catch for 22 yards to start the Seahawks' next possession. A pass-interference penalty on the Cowboys put the Seahawks at the Dallas 25 with 1:40 left. Two plays later, Hasselbeck hit D.J. Hackett at the 1-yard line. Then it was Hasselbeck to tight end Ryan Hannam for the touchdown to tie the game with 40 seconds to play.

Three plays into the Cowboys' final drive, Babineaux made his interception, and Brown made his kick and his plans for the victory celebration. But another Seahawk was way ahead of him.

"I'm over there signaling 'It's good' before he even got on the field," said running back Shaun Alexander. "I am Mr. Optimistic." ∎

Jordan Babineaux (27) returns an interception for 25 yards to set up the winning field goal by Josh Brown.
Seattle's Kelly Herndon is at left, and the intended Dallas receiver, Terry Glenn, is sprawled on the ground behind.

SEAHAWKS

33

CARDINALS

19

SCORING

Seattle	3	14	10	6	33
Arizona	3	3	10	3	19

HAWK HIGHLIGHTS

RB Shaun Alexander:
23 carries, 173 yards, 2 TD

QB Matt Hasselbeck:
13-20, 158 yards, TD

KR Josh Scobey:
6 returns, 27.5 yards avg.

FS Marquand Manuel:
12 tackles, one pass defense

DE Bryce Fisher:
3 tackles, 2 sacks, 2 pass
defenses, forced fumble

BY THE NUMBERS

0—Seahawks turnovers
4—Arizona turnovers

EXTRA POINTS

Seattle's defensive backfield
intercepted three passes, and
free safety Marquand Manuel
led the team in tackles.

Tummy ache, jinx and Cardinals no match for Seattle

No stopping
the Seahawks

Shaun Alexander had a big afternoon, outrunning the Cardinals defense for an 88-yard touchdown in the third quarter.

Nothing could stop the Seahawks, not a player's upset stomach, not a coach's jinx and certainly not the Arizona Cardinals, who lost 33-19 at Sun Devil Stadium.

The upset stomach was Shaun Alexander's.

"Just a little tummy ache," the Seattle running back said. "The first half was just rough. Every time I was tackled I felt like I was either going to throw up or go the other way. Sometimes you're not at your best, but you just keep on going."

He went into the locker room for treatment with just less than four minutes left in the first half and came out feeling much better in the second half, running 88 yards for a touchdown on the first play from scrimmage. That tied his team record for the longest run from scrimmage.

The coach's jinx was Mike Holmgren's, who had a streak of six consecutive losses after bye weeks as Seattle's coach.

"I am now 1-0 after the bye. Starting a new ➤

Bryce Fisher, left, and Mike Holmgren wore big smiles as they left Sun Devil Stadium after Seattle beat Arizona.

"
We're coming at you.
What you have to do is
stop it. Good luck."

— SEAHAWKS OFFENSIVE TACKLE
WALTER JONES

After missing three games
with cracked ribs, Seahawks
receiver Bobby Engram, left,
returned to catch three
passes for 24 yards,

Seahawks defensive tackle Chuck Darby, left, chases Cardinals quarterback Kurt Warner out of the pocket in the first half. Warner was sacked four times and threw three interceptions.

➤ streak," he joked.

Holmgren had given his players a week off after their 13-10 win over Dallas.

"We were a little bit sore and banged up and they played well, they earned it, so why not?" Holmgren said. "To their credit, they came back and prepared well for this football game."

The win, their fourth straight, improved the Seahawks' record to 6-2.

Despite his tummy troubles, Alexander played a big part, tearing through the Cardinals for a season-high 173 rushing yards on 23 carries. He scored two touchdowns to give him 14 on the season.

His third-quarter touchdown gave the Seahawks a 24-6 lead. Although Arizona made it interesting by cutting the lead to 27-19 with 12:09 left in the fourth quarter, the Seahawks drove 93 yards, and Alexander's second touchdown finished off the Cardinals.

Quarterback Matt Hassellbeck ran for a touchdown and threw for another to Joe Jurevicius. Josh Brown added two field goals, but his last extra-point attempt was blocked.

Three Seattle defensive backs had interceptions: Marcus Trufant, Kelly Herndon and Jordan Babineaux. "We've been saying we have to get more turnovers," cornerback Andre Dyson said. "(Today) we did, and it feels good." ■

SEAHAWKS

31

RAMS

16

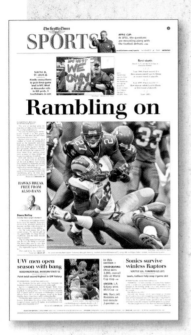

SCORING

St. Louis	3	0	6	7	16
Seattle	0	10	14	7	31

HAWK HIGHLIGHTS

RB Shaun Alexander:
33 carries, 165 yards, 3 TD

QB Matt Hasselbeck:
17-29, 243 yards, TD, 2 IN

LB Leroy Hill:
4 tackles, sack

BY THE NUMBERS

60% — Seattle red-zone efficiency

20% — Rams red-zone efficiency

EXTRA POINTS

Shaun Alexander's three touchdowns gave him 17 for the season, the first player in NFL history with at least 15 TDs in five consecutive seasons. He also went over the 1,000-yard mark for the fifth time in his career, setting a Seahawks record.

Lorin Sandretzky says it all for the fans as the Seahawks soundly defeated St. Louis to claim a commanding lead in the NFC West.

Seahawks make it a Ram sweep

Game gives them "powerhouse" status

The Seahawks have arrived as an NFL powerhouse.

Any doubt about that was erased with the 31-16 dismantling of the St. Louis Rams as 67,192 fans watched in the November rain and cold of Qwest Field.

At 7-2, the Seahawks share the NFC's best record with Carolina. Their fifth straight win gives them a three-game lead in the NFC West over the 4-5 Rams with only seven games left to play in the regular season. The last time the Seahawks were 7-2 was in 1999, coach Mike Holmgren's first season.

The Seahawks won the West in 2004, but fell to the Rams twice in the regular season and were eliminated by them in the first round of the playoffs. This year, Seattle makes it a regular-season sweep.

Leading the way for the Seahawks? Shaun Alexander, of course. He had 165 yards on 33 carries and scored three touchdowns.

Seattle led 10-3 at halftime and then put together back-to-back touchdown drives for a 24-6 lead. Alexander highlighted the first drive with a 37-yard run and ➤

Fellow wideouts Bobby Engram (84) and D.J. Hackett celebrate after Hackett's third-quarter touchdown reception — his first in the NFL.

In his best day as a receiver, D.J. Hackett makes a 47-yard catch in the second quarter to set up a Shaun Alexander touchdown.

Seattle's Jordan Babineaux (27), Leroy Hill and Bryce Fisher, bottom, bring down St. Louis running back Steven Jackson in the second quarter. Jackson was held to 70 yards.

> "
> It's a really cool thing when you can see the changing of the guard, and you're the new big dog on the scene."
>
> — RUNNING BACK
> SHAUN ALEXANDER

➤ finished it with a 4-yard smash into the end zone.

Matt Hasselbeck hit wide receiver D.J. Hackett in stride for a 31-yard touchdown pass in the second drive.

With 8:35 remaining in the game and trailing 24-9, the Rams drove 46 yards in four plays to score, pulling them within eight, 24-16.

The Seahawks took possession with 6:53 left, and the Rams couldn't stop them. They especially couldn't stop Alexander, who scored on a 17-yard run with 1:12 left in the game.

Alexander became the only player in NFL history to score 15 touchdowns in five consecutive seasons.

"I'm a better running back every time I step on the field," Alexander said, "and if I'm not, then I'm not doing our team any justice."

The defense allowed only one touchdown, forced two turnovers and sacked Rams quarterback Marc Bulger three times.

"Going out and sweeping them and maybe putting their playoff hopes away means a lot to us," defensive end Grant Wistrom said. ■

Seahawks tight end Jerramy Stevens tries to leap over St. Louis' Dexter Coakley (52) in the second quarter.

SEAHAWKS
27

49ERS
25

SCORING

Seattle	3	14	10	0	27
San Francisco	3	6	3	13	25

HAWK HIGHLIGHTS

RB Shaun Alexander:
24 carries, 115 yards, 2 TD

QB Matt Hasselbeck:
19-31, 233 yards, TD

WR Bobby Engram:
6 catches, 93 yards

LB D.D. Lewis:
8 tackles

DT Rocky Bernard:
5 tackles, 2 sacks

BY THE NUMBERS

3—Seahawks dropped passes

TURNING POINT

Fumble recovery by Seahawks Josh Scobey with 3:45 left in the third quarter. It set up the Seattle field goal that gave them a 27-12 lead and ultimately forced the 49ers to go unsuccessfully for two in the closing seconds.

Seahawks show they can finish

A scare in San Francisco, but a win in the end

I s this supposed to happen to powerhouses? One week after sweeping the St. Louis Rams in regular-season games and saying they felt they had arrived as an NFL powerhouse, the Seattle Seahawks came two points from likely having to go overtime against the lowly San Francisco 49ers.

The 27-25 escape against the 49ers (2-8) at Monster Park was a lesson for Seattle: even good teams can struggle. The difference in 2005 from years past is that those struggles haven't led to crushing losses, but to uplifting wins.

"We're very happy to get out of here with a win," said quarterback Matt Hasselbeck. "In fact, I heard someone in the locker room say, 'Let's get out of here before they change the score.' ...Good teams overcome that adversity."

The Seahawks have an 8-2 record for the first time since 1999 and six straight wins for the first time since 1984.

But San Francisco only fell short of sending the game into overtime when it failed on a two-point conversion attempt with 28 seconds remaining. The try for a tie came after San Francisco running back Maurice Hicks plunged in for a 1-yard touchdown run.

Seattle safety Marquand Manuel caught the 49ers' ensuing onside kick, got belted and still hung on to the ball. Only then did the Seahawks celebrate.

"That's the one that counts!" Manuel shouted after returning to the sideline.

Running back Shaun Alexander rushed for 115 yards and scored two more touchdowns to give him 19 on the season. Receivers Bobby Engram, D.J. Hackett and Joe Jurevicius ➤

Seahawks defensive backs Michael Boulware (28) and Kelly Herndon celebrate 49ers receiver Johnnie Morton's (84) missed catch on a two-point try with 28 seconds left.

➤ combined for 16 catches, and Hackett hauled in a 12-yard touchdown pass in the second quarter. Kicker Josh Brown added two field goals.

The Seahawks led 27-12 at one point in the second half, but did not make a first down in the fourth quarter.

Until San Francisco's two touchdowns in the fourth quarter, the Seattle defense had held the 49ers to four field goals. The Seahawks had four sacks of San Francisco quarterback Ken Dorsey, two by defensive tackle Rocky Bernard.

"We're all working together," defensive tackle Chuck Darby said. "They played us tough… They came out shooting, and we had to shoot back." ■

Defensive tackle Rocky Bernard delivers a punishing blow to 49ers quarterback Ken Dorsey in the second half.

It was a tough day for Rodney Bailey and the Seahawks defense as the 49ers took the game down to the final minute.

SEAHAWKS

24

OVERTIME

21

GIANTS

L W W L W W W W W W W ○ ○ ○ ○ ○

Seattle gets a leg up

N.Y. kicker misses three tries; Brown hits for the win

Seahawks kicker Josh Brown is congratulated after his overtime field goal extended Seattle's win streak.

Giants kicker Jay Feely (2) walks dejectedly off the field after missing a 40-yard field-goal attempt that would have given New York the win in regulation.

SCORING

					OT	
New York	0	10	3	8	0	21
Seattle	7	0	7	7	3	24

HAWK HIGHLIGHTS

WR Joe Jurevicius:
8 catches, 137 yards, 2 TD

RB Shaun Alexander:
31 carries, 110 yards, TD

QB Matt Hasselbeck:
21-37, 249 yards, 2 TD, IN

Punter Tom Rouen:
9 punts, 45. 6 average

BY THE NUMBERS

65—Yards Seattle penalized
114—Yards New York penalized

TURNING POINTS

You could say each time Giants kicker Jay Feely missed a field goal, any of which would have won the game. He was 2 for 5 on the night.

Crowd noise seemed to affect the Giants who were flagged for 11 false starts.

90

The outcome came down to the kickers. Jay Feely had three chances to win the game for the New York Giants. His 40-yard field-goal attempt to win in regulation sailed wide left. His 54-yard try at the 10:48 mark in overtime came up well short. His 45-yard effort with 6:05 left in overtime was also short.

All the while, Seahawks kicker Josh Brown stood on the sideline, waiting his chance. Finally, with just over three minutes left in overtime, the Seahawks got into field-goal range, and Brown's 36-yard kick split the uprights for a 24-21 overtime victory against one of the best teams Seattle had faced.

It was the seventh win in a row for the Seahawks, who remained the NFC's top team with a 9-2 record. The victory kept alive Seattle's hopes of getting into the playoffs with home-field advantage throughout and ➤

New York's Jay Feely misses a second field-goal attempt — this one in overtime. He would miss once more before Seattle's Josh Brown made his winning kick.

on Giants

> **"** You can't keep giving a good team like Seattle opportunities to move down the field… They have a good kicker, and they got in there and made it."
>
> — GIANTS KICKER JAY FEELY

Joe Jurevicius signals a touchdown after reeling in a 35-yard touchdown pass from Matt Hasselbeck — one of two on the day.

➤ moved the team to one win from the NFC West title.

The Seahawks led 21-13 at the 4:33 mark of the fourth quarter after Shaun Alexander burst through the line on fourth-and-inches from the Giants' 4-yard line for a touchdown.

But the Giants mounted a quick eight-play, 61-yard drive, capped by Eli Manning's 18-yard touchdown pass to Amani Toomer to get to 21-19 with 1:59 left in regulation. Manning hit tight end Jeremy Shockey for the game-tying two-point conversion.

The Seahawks' decisive overtime drive included a 38-yard pass from Matt Hasselbeck to D.J.

Hackett. That was followed by two Alexander runs of 8 and 13 yards to set up Brown's field goal.

Wide receiver Joe Jurevicius accounted for Seattle's other two touchdowns and caught eight passes for 137 yards.

The defense gave up chunks of yards to Giants running back Tiki Barber and on Manning's passes to Shockey and receiver Plaxico Burress. The Giants, who fell to 7-4, gained 490 yards of offense, by far the most the Seahawks have allowed.

"A lot of yards, a few points," Seahawks linebacker Lofa Tatupu said. "I'd rather have it that way than the other way." ∎

Seahawks receiver D.J. Hackett dances after catching a 38-yard pass that put Seattle close to field-goal range in overtime. He finished with two receptions for 47 yards.

New York tight end Jeremy Shockey bobbles the ball in overtime as Andre Dyson (21) and Leroy Hill defend. Officials ruled that Shockey had made the catch, then fumbled, and they spotted the ball at the 20-yard line. After reviewing the play, they ruled it an incomplete pass and moved the ball back to the 36.

SEAHAWKS
42

EAGLES
0

SCORING

Seattle	14	21	7	0	**42**
Philadelphia	0	0	0	0	**0**

HAWK HIGHLIGHTS

CB Andre Dyson:
INT, fumble recovery, 2TD

LB Lofa Tatupu:
9 tackles, INT, TD

LB Leroy Hill:
6 tackles, 1.5 sacks, FF

RB Shaun Alexander:
19 carries, 49 yards, 2 TD

QB Matt Hasselbeck:
8-15, 98 yards, TD

BY THE NUMBERS

0—Seattle turnovers
6—Philadelphia turnovers
3—Defensive touchdowns
for the Seahawks

EXTRA POINTS

The Seahawks won the NFC
West for the second straight
season and have now won
four division titles, including
those in 1988 and 1999.

94

Seattle defense scores 3 times

Eagles can't score against Seahawks

The Seahawks defense owned this Monday night game, a 42-0 shutout of the defending NFC champion Philadelphia Eagles in the driving snow at Lincoln Financial Field.

The defense had four interceptions and returned two of them for touchdowns. The Seahawks forced two fumbles and returned one for a score. They held the Eagles to 190 total yards, and, oh yeah, they kept Philadelphia out of the end zone.

The Seahawks came into the game knowing they had clinched the NFC West and a playoff spot after the St. Louis Rams lost on Sunday. Seattle's goal now was the best record in the conference, which would mean a first-round bye and home-field advantage throughout the playoffs.

Seattle got a step closer at accomplishing that. The 10-2 Seahawks won their eighth straight game, tying a franchise record set in 1984.

The Seahawks' top-ranked offense set the tone early with a 16-play, 65-yard touchdown drive. With 6:59 left in the first quarter, wide receiver Bobby Engram caught an 11-yard touchdown pass from quarterback Matt Hasselbeck.

Andre Dyson gave the Seahawks a 14-0 lead with 3:38 left in the first quarter when he intercepted Eagles quarterback Mike McMahon and returned it 72 yards for a touchdown.

In the second quarter, rookie linebacker Lofa Tatupu picked off another McMahon pass and ran it 38 yards for a touchdown.

Seattle built its halftime lead to 35-0 on two short-yard touchdown runs by Shaun Alexander. Safety Michael Boulware set up the first one when he intercepted a pass tipped by Tatupu and ran it 32 yards to the Philadelphia 2-yard line. The second Alexander run came after a 42-yard pass to D.J. Hackett, who brought the ball down despite double coverage at the Philadelphia 3.

On the first play from scrimmage in the second half, Seahawks linebacker Leroy Hill stripped running back Ryan Moats of the ball. Dyson picked it up and ran 25 yards for the score, becoming the first Seahawk since Dave Brown in 1984 to score two defensive touchdowns in a game.

"We finally put a game together, and we have been looking for that for a while," Dyson said. "We did it on a big stage and showed how good we were as a defense."

Seahawks rookie Lofa Tatupu (51) steps in front of Philadelphia receiver L.J. Smith for an interception in the second quarter. Tatupu returned the ball 38 yards for a touchdown.

FOLLOWING PAGES: The snow fell heavily by the end of the Seahawks' 42-0 win over the Philadelphia Eagles. It was the largest margin of victory in a shutout in Monday Night Football history

4:12 QTR 4 EAGLE

SEAHAWKS

41

49ERS

3

SCORING

San Francisco	3	0	0	0	3
Seattle	7	17	14	3	41

HAWK HIGHLIGHTS

QB Matt Hasselbeck:
21-25, 226 yards, 4 TD, IN

RB Shaun Alexander:
21 carries, 108 yards, TD

WR Bobby Engram
6 catches, 65 yards, 2 TD

LB Lofa Tatupu
INT, sack, fumble recover

BY THE NUMBERS

438—Seattle total yards
113—Philadelphia total yards

EXTRA POINTS

Rocky Bernard started at defensive tackle and made five tackles. Marcus Tubbs, who has been nursing a calf injury, came off the bench and made four tackles, two sacks and forced a fumble.

49ers not even close this time

Seahawks complete sweep of NFC West foes

The San Francisco 49ers didn't come close this time.

In November they took the Seahawks down to the closing seconds in San Francisco, and Seattle escaped with a 27-25 win by thwarting a two-point conversion try.

But at Qwest Field in front of 66,690 fans, the Seahawks dominated the 49ers, 41-3, for their first division sweep (6-0) of NFC West opponents, their first nine-game winning streak in franchise history and an 11-2 record that put them on top of the NFC.

With three games left in the regular season, Seattle can clinch the conference's best record and home-field advantage throughout the playoffs with two wins, or with one win and a loss by the 9-4 Chicago Bears.

Seattle scored on the first possession of the game, a 28-yard pass play from Matt Hasselbeck to Bobby Engram, his first of two touchdowns in the game.

San Francisco got the ball and managed a 39-yard field goal by Joe Nedney, the only 49er score of the game.

At halftime, the Seahawks had a 24-3 lead after wide receiver Joe Jurevicius ripped the ball from San Francisco cornerback Shawntae Spencer in the end zone for a touchdown, tight end Jerramy Stevens gathered in an 8-yard pass for a score and Josh Brown hit his first of two 52-yard field goals.

Shaun Alexander rushed for 108 yards on 21 carries and scored a touchdown before leaving the game after three quarters. This was his ninth 100-yard game of the season, breaking Chris Warren's team record of eight set in 1995.

Hasselbeck completed 21 of 25 passes for ➤

Cornerback Jordan Babineaux leaps into the appreciative crowd in Qwest Field's south end zone after the Seahawks wrapped up their rout of the 49ers.

Lofa Tatupu heads upfield for 14 yards after
intercepting a 49er pass in the second quarter.

➤ 226 yards and four touchdowns.

Seattle's offense racked up 438 yards while
their defense held San Francisco to just 113. The
three points allowed in the past two games are
the lowest total over back-to-back games since
1984, when the Seahawks shut out San Diego and
Kansas City.

"It feels like we're on this ride right now,"
Alexander said, "and nobody wants to see it
stopped." ■

Joe Jurevicius points to the crowd with
the football after catching a 21-yard
touchdown pass in the second quarter,
giving the Seahawks a 21-3 lead.

It feels like we're on this ride right now, and nobody wants to see it stopped."

— RUNNING BACK
SHAUN ALEXANDER

Seattle kicker
Josh Brown
screams with joy
after making his
second 52-yard
field goal in
the game.

SEAHAWKS

28

TITANS

24

L W W L W W W W W W W W W W W

Seattle kicker Josh Brown knocks the helmet off Tennessee's Rich Gardner as the two players scramble for the ball after Tennessee blocked Brown's field-goal attempt in the second quarter.

Nothing comes easy in the NFL

Comeback victory earns playoff bye

Seattle's 10th straight regular-season win means they won't have to play in the first round of the playoffs. But winning that bye did not come easy.

The Tennessee Titans scored 24 unanswered points to take a 10-point lead deep into the third quarter before Seahawks quarterback Matt Hasselbeck spearheaded a 28-24 comeback win at The Coliseum. Two fourth-down stands by the defense and some tough running by Shaun Alexander also helped save the day for Seattle.

The Seahawks 12-2 record means they will be one of the top two seeds in the NFC playoffs. With two regular-season games left to play, they need one more win or a loss by the Chicago Bears to clinch home-field advantage throughout the postseason.

For the third week in a row, the Seahawks had a game-opening touchdown drive, scoring on a 22-yard pass from Hasselbeck to Jerramy Stevens.

Alexander's 52-yard run on the Seahawks' next possession was the highlight of a six-play, 79-yard drive that ended in Alexander's ➤

SCORING

Seattle	14	0	7	7	28
Tennessee	0	14	10	0	24

HAWK HIGHLIGHTS

QB Matt Hasselbeck:
21-27, 285 yards, 3 TD

RB Shaun Alexander:
26 carries, 172 yards, TD

WR Bobby Engram:
6 catches, 95 yards, TD

SS Michael Boulware:
10 tackles

BY THE NUMBERS

459—Seattle total yards
417—Tennessee total yards

EXTRA POINTS

WR Darrell Jackson started for the first time since week four and arthroscopic knee surgery. He had 6 catches for 72 yards and a touchdown.

Shaun Alexander became only the fifth player in NFL history to rush for 1,600 yards in consecutive seasons.

"

We can't really celebrate this victory very long. It was a big win for us, but it was ugly. We have a lot to learn from it."

— SAFETY MICHAEL BOULWARE

Seahawks defenders Jimmy Williams (22) and Lofa Tatupu celebrate after stopping the Titans' final drive on fourth-and-two in the fourth quarter.

Seattle fans in Nashville wave banners and signs as the Seahawks leave the Coliseum after beating the Tennessee Titans, 28-24.

Matt Hasselbeck goes over formations with his receivers, trying to get the Seattle offense moving in the second and third quarters.

Seahawks receiver Bobby Engram (84) looks for yardage despite the efforts of the Titans' Lamont Thompson in the first half. Engram had six catches for a team-high 95 yards.

➤ 1-yard touchdown run.

Then Tennessee got going.

With 6:08 left in the first half, Jarrett Payton scored on a 3-yard run, the first offensive touchdown in three weeks for the 4-10 Titans.

With eight seconds left in the half, an 84-yard drive culminated with Titans quarterback Steve McNair hitting wide receiver Drew Bennett for a touchdown to tie the score.

Tennessee opened the second half by driving 78 yards for another touchdown, a 14-yard pass from McNair to Bennett.

Down 24-14 with 6:07 left in the third quarter, the Seahawks woke up. Bobby Engram gained 56 yards on a

pass play. Darrell Jackson, back from an injury after a 10-game absence, picked up 23 more. Then Hasselbeck found Joe Jurevicius for a 4-yard touchdown pass, his team-high ninth touchdown catch of the season.

Tennessee failed to pick up a first down on a fourth-down gamble, and the Seahawks marched 93 yards for the go-ahead score, Hasselbeck to Jackson from 2 yards out.

The defense stopped Tennessee once more in a fourth-down situation, and Seattle took over and ran out the clock.

Alexander's 172-yard performance was only a yard short of his best effort of the season, and Hasselbeck passed for 285 yards, completing all but six of 27 throws. ∎

SEAHAWKS

28

COLTS

13

SCORING

Indianapolis	3	3	0	7	13
Seattle	7	7	7	7	28

HAWK HIGHLIGHTS

RB Shaun Alexander:
21 carries, 139 yards, 3 TD

QB Matt Hasselbeck:
17-21, 168 yards, 2 TD

CB Jordan Babineaux:
12 tackles

DT Marcus Tubbs:
6 tackles, sack,
forced fumble

BY THE NUMBERS

6-15-40% Colts third-down
efficiency
1-7-14% Seahawks third-
down efficiency

EXTRA POINTS

With four touchdowns in the
game, the Seahawks have
55, the most they've scored
in a season. The previous
record was 51 in 1984.

Ⓛ Ⓦ Ⓦ Ⓛ Ⓦ Ⓦ Ⓦ Ⓦ Ⓦ Ⓦ Ⓦ Ⓦ Ⓦ Ⓦ Ⓦ

Seattle is home

Win over Colts makes Seahawks NFC's best

The Seahawks could have waited around to see if the Chicago Bears lost to get home-field advantage throughout the playoffs. But why wait when there's a more direct route?

The Seahawks took that route by defeating the Indianapolis Colts 28-13 at Qwest Field, assuring themselves of the best record (13-2) and top playoff seed in the NFC with one more regular-season game to play.

The victory — their 11th straight — gave the Seahawks 13 regular season wins for the first time in the 30-year history of the franchise. They finished undefeated at home (8-0) for the second time in the past three seasons and set a club record with 55 season touchdowns.

The Colts already had the best record in the AFC (also 13-2 after the Seattle loss) and rested several starters. Seahawks coach Mike Holmgren said he might follow suit in the last game of the regular season since Seattle has won top playoff positioning and could use an extra week for some players to nurse injuries.

Some were already talking that the Seahawks might face the Colts in the Super Bowl.

"Hopefully we'll face them again," said Seattle defensive end Grant Wistrom. "They've got a good shot at getting there and hopefully we do, too. We'll probably have to face them full force at some point."

The Colts started the scoring with a field goal by Mike Vanderjagt. The Seahawks scored a touchdown on their opening drive — the first of three TDs for Shaun Alexander.

Then Seattle blocked a Colts field-goal attempt and turned that into a second touchdown drive, this one ending in a 15-yard strike from Matt Hasselbeck to tight end Jerramy Stevens.

The Seahawks took a 28-6 lead in dramatic fashion. With 3:58 left in the game, Alexander came off the bench to the delight of the 67,855 fans, aware that his next touchdown would give him 27 on the season and tie the NFL single-season record, set in 2003 by Priest Holmes of Kansas City. Alexander scored from a yard out.

Defensively, the Seahawks disrupted the Colts passing game and held them to 43 rushing yards, the lowest total allowed by the Seahawks defense all season.

> **"** Hopefully we'll face them again. They've got a good shot at getting there and hopefully we do, too. We'll probably have to face them full force at some point."
>
> — DEFENSIVE END GRANT WISDOM

for the playoffs

Seahawks coach Mike Holmgren, right, tries to escape a celebratory dunking courtesy of center Robbie Tobeck as the clock winds down in the Seahawks 28-13 victory over the Indianapolis Colts.

Seattle wide receiver Bobby Engram encourages cheers from the crowd after he led the team back onto the field to thank fans afterward.

Seahawks and Colts pray after the game for the family of Indianapolis coach Tony Dungy, whose 18-year-old son died earlier in the week.

Some of the 67,855 fans at Qwest Field cheer Matt Hasselbeck as he waits in the special-effects smoke before his introduction.

Shaun Alexander sprints around Colts defenders Gilbert Gardner and Josh Williams (96). Alexander had 139 yards and three touchdowns. With 27 touchdowns in the season, Alexander tied the NFL single-season record.

PACKERS

23

SEAHAWKS

17

L W W L W W W W W W W W W W W L

Coach Mike Holmgren, who took the Packers to two Super Bowls before coming to Seattle, congratulates Green Bay quarterback Brett Favre after the game.

Seahawks lose but get what they want

Alexander sets TD record, tops the NFL in rushing

The Seahawks lost 23-17 to the Green Bay Packers in the game at Lambeau Field, but in the big picture, they got what they wanted.

They rested starters.

They avoided injuries.

Their backups got playing time.

And they secured the NFL single-season touchdown record and the 2005 NFL rushing title for running back Shaun Alexander.

The loss meant an end to the franchise-record, 11-game win streak, but the Seahawks still ended the season with the best mark in team history, a 13-3 record.

Now they sit out a week while the wild-card teams play to see who comes to Qwest Field for the NFC divisional playoffs.

"We did some good things, but now our second season starts," said coach Mike Holmgren. "Fortunately we have a first-round bye, and we can heal up a little bit."

Alexander scored his 28th touchdown of the season with 13 minutes left in the second quarter, breaking the NFL single-season mark of 27 set by Kansas City's Priest Holmes in 2003.

Alexander's 3-yard gain with 1:14 left in the half was enough to give him his first NFL rushing title.

"We wanted him to have the record, he wanted to have the ➤

SCORING

Seattle	0	7	7	3	17
Green Bay	6	7	7	3	23

HAWK HIGHLIGHTS

RB Shaun Alexander:
20 carries, 73 yards, TD
Set NFL single-season TD record and clinched season rushing title with 1,880 yards.

CB Jordan Babineaux
11 tackles

CB Jimmy Williams
9 tackles, INT

BY THE NUMBERS

35:13 — Packers time of possession
24:47 — Seahawks time of possession

EXTRA POINTS

Shaun Alexander fumbled in the second quarter and Green Bay recovered, Alexander's first lost fumble of the season. The Seahawks only lost seven all season.

Shaun Alexander gains 5 yards in the final Seahawks drive of the second quarter. By the end of the drive, he had enough yards to secure the 2005 NFL rushing title.

➤ record, the linemen wanted the record for him," Holmgren said, "and so, in the first half we were playing to get him the ball and the record."

The Packers didn't make it easy, holding Alexander to 17 first-quarter yards on five carries.

"They were determined to stop him from getting his yards," tackle

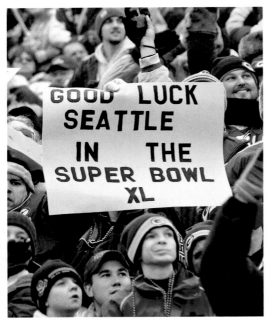

Shaun Alexander strolls into the end zone on a 1-yard run at Lambeau Field and points to the heavens, celebrating his NFL-record 28th touchdown of the season.

Sean Locklear said. "It's huge. We secured it."

Alexander finished with 20 carries for 73 yards and did not play in the second half, ending the season with 1,880 yards.

The defense gave up first downs on 11 of 20 Packers third downs.

"It's been a long time since we've had to go in on Monday and be afraid of what we saw on tape," said Bryce Fisher, Seattle defensive end. "But it actually may end up working for us in that we'll get to recognize that we can't just be out there going through the motions. We need to play with the fire and intensity that's carried us through the season." ∎

SEAHAWKS' 2006 PRO BOWL PLAYERS

LOFA TATUPU	ROBBIE TOBECK	MATT HASSELBECK	MACK STRONG	SHAUN ALEXANDER	STEVE HUTCHINSON	WALTER JONES
LINEBACKER	CENTER	QUARTERBACK	FULLBACK	RUNNING BACK	LEFT GUARD	LEFT TACKLE

⭐ *FIRST TEAM ALL PRO*

Hawks show star power

Seven Seahawks were invited to play in the Pro Bowl; A team-record four were voted to the All-Pro team

For the first time in team history, four Seahawks were voted onto the NFL's All-Pro first team: Walter Jones, Steve Hutchinson, Shaun Alexander and Mack Strong.

Those four plus three other Seahawks were also invited to play in the Pro Bowl. Quarterback Matt Hasselbeck received his invitation when the teams were announced in December. Center Robbie Tobeck and middle linebacker Lofa Tatupu, who had both been named as alternates, were added to the team after the NFC Championship Game in January. That puts seven Seahawks on the NFC team for the Feb. 12 game, played in Hawaii one week after the Super Bowl.

The Associated Press All-Pro selections come from 50 votes by a nationwide panel of sports writers and broadcasters who cover the NFL.

Players are voted on for the Pro Bowl, the NFL's all-star game, by the coaches, players and fans — each group counting for one third of the votes.

MACK STRONG
Fullback

His first selection as All Pro in his 13-year career. Strong, 34, signed with the Seahawks as a free agent in 1993 and was used on special teams early in his career. But for the past six years as fullback, he has blocked for running backs who have gained more than 1,000 yards a season. A letterman in football, basketball and track at Brookstone High School in Columbus, Ga., he played at Georgia, where he was a four-year letterman and two-year starter. He lives in Kirkland, and he and his wife Zoe have two children.

ROBBIE TOBECK
Center

A 13-year NFL veteran, Tobeck, 35, will be appearing in the first Pro Bowl of his career. Atlanta signed him as a free agent in May 1993 out of Washington State, where he started all 12 games at center for the 9-3 Cougar team his senior year. After he made Atlanta's active roster in 1994, he started five seasons for Atlanta, making the switch from guard to center in 1998 and played with them in Super Bowl XXXIII (Denver 34, Atlanta 19). He signed with the Seahawks in 2000. At 6 foot 4 and 297 pounds, he has started in 80 straight regular-season games. He lettered in both football and basketball at New Port Richie High School in Tarpon Springs, Fla. He is the father of four children.

115

STEVE HUTCHINSON
Left Guard

At 6 foot 5 and 313 pounds, Hutchinson matches up almost exactly with teammate Walter Jones. Hutchinson, 28, made first team All-Pro in 2003 and second team in 2004. The Seahawks selected him in the first round of the 2001 draft after a four-year-letter career at Michigan, where he earned first-team All Big Ten Conference honors four times and was first team All American his junior and senior years. Played football and basketball at Coral Springs (Fla.) High School and now lives in Key Largo, Fla., with wife Landyn.

SHAUN ALEXANDER Running Back

Alexander's (37) first selection as first-team All Pro after making second team in 2004. At 5 foot 11 and 225 pounds, he was the 2005 NFL Most Valuable Player and Offensive Player of the Year. He received 49 of 50 possible votes for first team All-Pro, and his Pro Bowl invitation is his third. Alexander, 28, was selected by the Seahawks in the first round of the 2000 NFL draft after four seasons at Alabama where he is the all-time rushing leader. His 110 touchdowns for Boone County (Ky.) High School ranks fifth on the prep national career-record list. He and his wife Valerie have two children.

WALTER JONES Left Tackle

At 6 foot 5 and 315 pounds, Jones (71) teams up with Steve Hutchinson to make perhaps the best left side in football. This is his third selection to the All-Pro first team and his sixth invitation to the Pro Bowl. Selected in the first round of the 1997 draft, the Florida State lineman earned first-team All-Rookie honors that year. In 1999, he became the first Seahawks lineman to play in the Pro Bowl. Jones, 32, grew up in Aliceville, Alabama, and he and his wife Valeria have three children.

MATT HASSELBECK Quarterback

Received his second invitation to the Pro Bowl after a regular season that saw him complete 65 percent of his passes (294-449) for 3,459 yards, 24 touchdowns and nine interceptions. Hasselbeck, 30, came to the Seahawks in a 2001 trade with Green Bay. The Packers, under then coach Mike Holmgren, made him a sixth-round choice in the 1998 draft. He was a four-year letterman and two-year starter at Boston College, and lettered in football, basketball and baseball at Xaverian Brothers High School in Westwood, Mass. He' s 6 foot 4 and weighs 223 pounds. He and his wife Sarah have two children.

LOFA TATUPU Middle Linebacker

A 6-foot, 238-pound rookie, he led the team in tackles with 105. The Seahawks selected Tatupu in the second round of the 2005 NFL draft. He became only the second player chosen from USC in Seahawks history (Kris Richard 2002). Tatupu, 23, transferred to USC after his freshman year at Maine and started 25 games in two years for the Trojans as they won back-to-back national championships. At King Phillip Regional High School in Wrentham, Mass., he played linebacker and quarterback, making 100 tackles and throwing for 800 yards and 10 TDs while rushing for 450 yards and five scores his senior year.

117

2006 SUPE

FIRST ROW (kneeling): Josh Brown, Matt Hasselbeck, David Greene, Tony Brown, Seneca Wallace, Tom Rouen, Maurice Mann, D.J. Hackett, Richard Smith, Maurice Morris, Andre Dyson, Jimmy Williams, Marcus Trufant, Jordan Babineaux, Ken Hamlin.
SECOND ROW: Michael Boulware, Marquis Weeks, Kelly Herndon, Marquand Manuel, Etric Pruitt, Shaun Alexander, Mack Strong, Josh Scobey, John Howell, Leonard Weaver, Cornelius Wortham, Lofa Tatupu, Jean-Philippe Darche, Niko Koutouvides, D.D. Lewis, Jamie Sharper.
THIRD ROW: Gary Reynolds, Keith Gilbertson, Bill Laveroni, Jim Lind, Stump Mitchell, Jim Zorn, Nolan Cromwell, Gil Haskell, Mike Holmgren, Paul Allen, Tim Ruskell, Tod Leiweke, Ray Rhodes, Dwaine Board, John Marshall, Teryl Austin, Zerick Rollins, Bob Casullo, John Jamison.

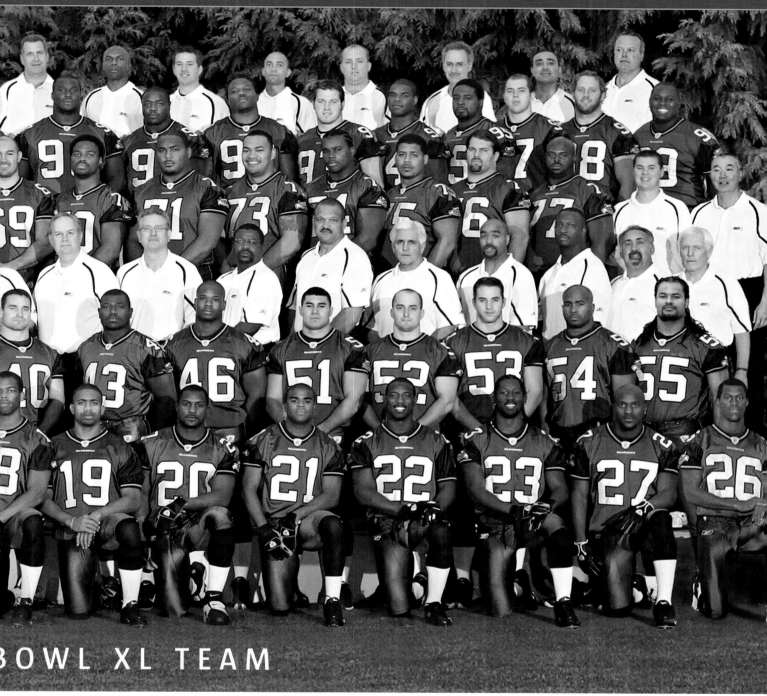

BOWL XL TEAM

FOURTH ROW: Mike Clark, Darren Krein, Leroy Hill, Kevin Bentley, Isaiah Kacyvenski, Robbie Tobeck, Chris Gray, Thatcher Szalay, Chris Spencer, Joe Tafoya, Nathaniel Adibi, Walter Jones, Wayne Hunter, Ray Willis, Sean Locklear, Steve Hutchinson, Floyd Womack, Tom Headlee, Jim Yoshida.

FIFTH ROW: Rick Ninomiya, Peter Warrick, Darrell Jackson, Ryan Hannam, Bobby Engram, Alex Bannister, Jerramy Stevens, Joe Jurevicius, Itula Mili, Jerheme Urban, Marcus Tubbs, Chuck Darby, Alain Kashama, Craig Terrill, Bryce Fisher, Rodney Bailey, Jeb Huckeba, Grant Wistrom, Rocky Bernard.

TOP ROW: Thom Fermstad, Brad Campbell, John Mallory, Mark McDaniel, Jeff Bower, Erik Kennedy, Bill Nayes, Maurice Kelly, Mike Reinfeldt, Will Lewis, Sam Ramsden, Reggie Barnes, Don Rich, Dr. Stan Herring, Dr. Ed Khalfayan, Dr. Kevin Auld.

Seattle head coach Mike Holmgren gestures and tries to make a point with officials in the Houston game.

Holmgren gets "tough"

The relationship between Mike Holmgren and Ray Rhodes goes way back, but by the first week in November, Holmgren decided he needed to get tough with his defensive coordinator. Rhodes would not be on the field for practice anytime soon, Holmgren decreed, and for the time being, he would not be in the coaches' box during games to help with calls.

"I am not going to fudge on that, and I am not going to let him fudge on that," Holmgren said.

Some terrible offense on Rhodes' part?

Not at all. Just Holmgren making sure Rhodes took care of himself after a second occurrence of stroke-like symptoms.

Holmgren said Rhodes had agreed to reduce his hours after his first episode in September but that Rhodes "was sneaking around on me."

"He cheated on me," Holmgren said. "So I'm going to walk in there every night around 5 o'clock and escort him to his car."

Holmgren asked Rhodes to step aside and let linebacker coach John Marshal call defensive signals. Marshall, in his 26th years as an NFL coach, had been a defensive coordinator for three teams — Atlanta, San Francisco and Carolina — and came to Seattle to be the linebackers coach in 2003.

He deflected credit for the success of the Seahawks' defense.

"This is Ray's defense, it's a staff deal," Marshall said. "That's the only way you can survive in the league. You gotta use all the minds you got, and that's what we're doing."

The top minds that helped the Seahawks survive and thrive this season included:

MIKE HOLMGREN

Seahawks head coach for seven years, he has posted winning records in five of those seasons while winning three division titles (1999, 2004 and 2005). He was head coach at Green Bay from 1992 to 1998 and took the Packers to the Super Bowl twice, including a 35-21 victory over the New England Patriots in Super Bowl XXXI. Holmgren was an assistant coach for the 49ers and coached at San Francisco State and BYU, where they won a national championship in 1984. He also coached at three high schools, including his alma mater, Lincoln High School in San Francisco, where he played quarterback as he did at USC.

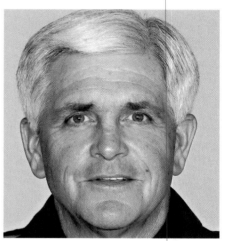

RAY RHODES

Joined the Seahawks as defensive coordinator in 2003. At Green Bay (1992-1993), Rhodes helped the Holmgren-led Packers to their first playoff appearance since 1982. Rhodes spent one season as a head coach at Green Bay in 1999 when the team went 8-8. In the 1970s, he played wide receiver and defensive back for the New York Giants before being traded to the San Francisco 49ers. In his 24 years as an NFL coach, Rhodes has also held positions for the 49ers, the Philadelphia Eagles, the Washington Redskins and the Denver Broncos.

GIL HASKELL

The team's offensive coordinator also worked under Holmgren at Green Bay in the 1990s. He joined the Seahawks in 2000 after serving as offensive coordinator for the Carolina Panthers (1998-99). Haskell entered the NFL in 1983 and served nine seasons with the Los Angeles Rams (1983-91). He also coached at USC (1978-1982) and at San Francisco's St. Ignatius High School (1969-77).

JOHN MARSHALL

He started the season as linebackers coach, then filled in as defensive coordinator when Rhodes had a mild stroke on Sept. 4 and suffered stroke-like symptoms again on Nov. 4. Marshall, who coached with Detroit, Carolina, San Francisco, Indianapolis, Atlanta and Green Bay, also coached at the college level at Oregon and USC.

Seahawks owner Paul Allen (left) congratulates CEO Tod Leiweke (center) and Tim Ruskell, president of football operations.

Allen saves game for Seattle

In 1996, the Seattle Seahawks were headquartered in a Residence Inn in Anaheim, Calif. Team equipment had been moved there, and players were to follow.

At least that was the plan of then-owner Ken Behring, a California real-estate developer who saw opportunity in the departure of the Los Angeles Rams for St. Louis.

The NFL had not approved the move and told Behring to get back to Seattle. King County sued to prevent the departure of the team from the county-owned Kingdome, where the Seahawks had played since their start in 1976. It was also the place Behring said needed to be leveled and rebuilt because of the potential of an earthquake there.

Negotiations began with a man who had made billions as co-founder of Microsoft. Paul Allen said he would buy the team under one condition: He wanted to build a new stadium with help from the public.

He spent $9 million for the cost of an election and on the campaign. Referendum 48 would cap public spending on the stadium at $300 million with Allen picking up another $130 million plus any cost overruns.

At the center of the deal was Bob Whitsitt, the self-described "suit-and-tie" guy for Allen.

"I tried to convince Ken that he'd either make $100 million on the deal, or he'd be headed for the promised land in Los Angeles," said Whitsitt, who would spend eight years as Seahawks president.

Washington voters passed the measure in June 1997, and Allen bought the Seahawks for $200 million. The Kingdome was imploded in March 2000, and the new facility – eventually named Qwest Field – rose in its place.

In 1999, Mike Holmgren, who had won a Super Bowl with the Green Bay Packers, was signed to an eight-year deal as the Seahawks' coach and general manager. In his first season, he took the Seahawks to the playoffs, but that was it for four seasons.

In 2002, Holmgren cut back his front-office responsibilities to concentrate on coaching. CEO Tod Leiweke was hired in 2003 to make the Seahawks experience better for fans, something he had done for professional hockey's Minnesota Wild.

But after a disappointing 2004 playoff loss, it was clear not all was well. Within a week of the loss, Allen fired Whitsitt and brought in as president Tim Ruskell, who started as a football scout in the mid-1970s and had been working as Atlanta's assistant general manager.

Several new defensive players were brought in, contracts were completed with free agents and the Seahawks were on their way to Super Bowl XL, a long way from the Residence Inn in Anaheim.

Extraordinary fans reveal their true colors

Game Faces

PORTRAITS BY ROD MAR
Seattle Times staff photographer

In his everyday life, Bruce McMillan of Fife, is a cable splicer for Qwest…

…but on game day, in the south end zone of Qwest Field, he is "Painted Hawk." He's been a fan since 1978.

"CANNONBALL"

Brad Carter of Bonney Lake works
as a line technician for Comcast,
but at Qwest Field he is "Cannonball."
His most coveted memorabilia:
"A photo of Matt Hasselbeck and me
showing off our bald heads!"

"KILTMAN"

Neil Hart, Everett, a production worker at
Kimberley-Clark, is just another face
except when he is "Kiltman," sporting a
wild wig and a kilt in Seahawks colors.
He says he has been a fan since the
founding of the team in 1976
when he was 4 years old.

"Mr. and Mrs. Seahawk"

Jeff and DeDe Schumaier of Auburn are an everyday couple six days of the week; he's a truck driver and she's a waitress.
But on Seahawks game days they are "Mr. and Mrs. Seahawk," Seattle's first couple of pro football. They were married in the center of the Kingdome field before a sold-out Seahawks game on Sept. 20, 1998.

"Bam Bam"

Paco Trayan, Mountlake Terrace, is an auto technician in north Seattle, but on game days he becomes "Bam Bam," the guy in the south end zone pounding on the stadium padding with both forearms, something he's done since the first season in Qwest Field.

"FANATIC"

Brandon Kickbush, Shoreline, distributes wine for Noble Wines during the week and on game days morphs into the "FANatic," known for his loud, foghorn-like "SEEEEEEA-HAAAAAWKS!" yell. He said the secret to face painting was to use sealant, which locks down one color before the next is applied. "This way they don't blend," he said. "Plus, the rain rolls right off."

Picturing the person behind the paint

BY ROD MAR / *Seattle Times staff photographer*

I see them every game day, as do you. The crazy, face-painted, wildly-costumed fans who inhabit the first few rows of the south end zone at Qwest Field. They are as much a part of a Seahawks game as the raising of the 12th Man flag before kickoff. They lean over the barrier surrounding the field, yelling, pounding, high-fiving and occasionally crying.

Any photographer new to Qwest Field heads straight towards them. How could you not? The color, the antics and the zeal with which these fans cheer is fun to shoot and easy as well.

However, to any photographer who shoots Seahawks games regularly, they become part of the background scenery, much like the cityscape that rises over the north end zone. That is to say, it's easy to take them for granted.

Last season, while showing a newcomer around during pregame, he asked me, "Who the hell are these people?" Which got me to thinking — Who are the people behind the facepaint? What do they look like in "real life?" What do they do the rest of the week?

And so I sought to find out. Got some names and phone numbers. Thought of innumerable ways to photograph them. Decided that contrasting the "two sides" of these fans would be best presented in a "formal portrait" setting — studio lighting and a nice backdrop.

When I look at these portraits, I see fans just like you — they are real people, with real jobs, who share a passion that unites them on Sundays in the fall.

I hope you enjoyed these photographs.

SEAHAWKS STATISTICS

Regular-season individual statistics

PASSING	CMP PCT	YDS	TD	INT	RATE
Hasselbeck	65.5	3,459	24	9	98.2
Wallace	52.0	173	1	1	70.9

RUSHING	ATT	YDS	AVG	LONG	TD
Alexander	370	1,880	5.1	88t	27
Morris	71	288	4.1	49	1
Hasselbeck	36	124	3.4	23	1
Weaver	17	80	4.7	24	0
Strong	17	78	4.6	16	0
Jackson	1	7	7.0	7	0
Warrick	1	5	5.0	5	0

RECEIVING	ATT	YDS	AVG	LONG	TD
Engram	67	778	11.6	56	3
Jurevicius	55	694	12.6	52	10
Stevens	45	554	12.3	35t	5
Jackson	38	482	12.7	48	3
Hackett	28	400	14.3	47	2
Strong	22	166	7.5	27	0
Alexander	15	78	5.2	9	1
Hannam	13	89	6.8	20	1
Warrick	11	180	16.4	42	0
Urban	7	151	21.6	46	0
Morris	5	48	9.6	20	0

PUNTING	ATT	YDS	AVG	LONG	BLK
Araguz	18	723	40.2	53	0
Rouen	61	2,539	41.6	62	0

PUNT RETURN	ATT	YDS	AVG	LONG	TD
Williams	24	139	5.8	24	0
Warrick	6	29	4.8	10	0

KICK RETURN	ATT	YDS	AVG	LONG	TD
Scobey	59	1,326	22.5	53	0
Morris	1	21	21.0	21	0

FIELD GOALS	1-19	20-29	30-39	40-49	50+
J. Brown	0/0	5/5	4/5	4/7	5/8

SACKS:

Fisher 9.0, Bernard 8.5, Hill 7.5, Tubbs 5.5, Tatupu 4.0, Wistrom 4.0, Darby 2.5, Boulware 2.0, Terrill 2.0, Tafoya 1.0, Trufant 1.0,

INTERCEPTIONS:

Boulware 4, Babineaux 3, Tatupu 3, Herndon 2, Williams 2, Dyson 1, Trufant 1

SEAHAWKS PLAYOFF ROSTER

NO.	PLAYER	POS.	HT.	WT.	AGE	COLLEGE
3	Josh Brown	K	6-0	202	26	Nebraska
8	Matt Hasselbeck	QB	6-4	223	30	Boston College
11	David Greene	QB	6-3	226	23	Georgia
15	Seneca Wallace	QB	5-11	196	25	Iowa St.
16	Tom Rouen	P	6-3	225	37	Colorado
18	D.J. Hackett	WR	6-2	199	24	Colorado
20	Maurice Morris	RB	5-11	202	26	Oregon
21	Andre Dyson	CB	5-10	183	26	Utah
22	Jimmy Williams	CB	5-11	190	26	Vanderbilt
23	Marcus Trufant	CB	5-11	199	25	Washington St.
25	Michael Harden	CB	5-11	190	24	Missouri
27	Jordan Babineaux	S	6-0	200	23	So. Arkansas
28	Michael Boulware	S	6-3	223	24	Florida St.
31	Kelly Herndon	CB	5-10	180	29	Toledo
33	Marquand Manuel	S	6-0	209	26	Florida
35	Etric Pruitt	S	6-0	196	24	So. Mississippi
37	Shaun Alexander	RB	5-11	225	28	Alabama
38	Mack Strong	FB	6-0	245	34	Georgia
39	Josh Scobey	RB	6-0	216	26	Kansas St.
43	Leonard Weaver	FB	6-0	251	23	Carson-Newman
50	Cornelius Wortham	LB	6-1	236	23	Alabama
51	Lofa Tatupu	LB	6-0	238	23	USC
52	Jean-Philippe Darche	LS	6-0	246	30	McGill
53	Niko Koutouvides	LB	6-2	244	24	Purdue
54	D.D. Lewis	LB	6-1	241	26	Texas
56	LeRoy Hill	LB	6-1	229	23	Clemson
57	Kevin Bentley	LB	6-1	240	26	Northwestern
58	Isaiah Kacyvenski	LB	6-1	252	28	Harvard
61	Robbie Tobeck	C	6-4	297	35	Washington St.
62	Chris Gray	G	6-4	308	35	Auburn
65	Chris Spencer	C	6-3	309	23	Mississippi
69	Joe Tafoya	DE	6-4	265	27	Arizona
71	Walter Jones	T	6-5	315	32	Florida St.
73	Wayne Hunter	T	6-5	303	24	Hawaii
74	Ray Willis	T	6-6	327	23	Florida St.
75	Sean Locklear	T	6-4	301	24	North Carolina St.
76	Steve Hutchinson	G	6-5	313	28	Michigan
77	Floyd Womack	T	6-4	330	27	Mississippi St.
78	Robert Pollard	DE	6-2	278	24	Texas Christian
81	Peter Warrick	WR	5-11	195	28	Florida St.
82	Darrell Jackson	WR	6-0	201	27	Florida
83	Ryan Hannam	TE	6-2	248	25	Northern Iowa
84	Bobby Engram	WR	5-10	188	32	Penn St.
86	Jerramy Stevens	TE	6-7	265	26	Washington
87	Joe Jurevicius	WR	6-5	230	31	Penn St.
88	Itula Mili	TE	6-4	260	32	Brigham Young
90	Marcus Tubbs	DT	6-3	320	24	Texas
91	Chuck Darby	DT	6-0	270	30	South Carolina St.
93	Craig Terrill	DT	6-3	287	25	Purdue
94	Bryce Fisher	DE	6-3	272	28	Air Force Academy
95	Rodney Bailey	DL	6-3	305	26	Ohio St.
98	Grant Wistrom	DE	6-4	272	29	Nebraska
99	Rocky Bernard	DT	6-3	293	26	Texas A&M

CREDITS:

SPORTS EDITOR: Cathy Henkel

BOOK DESIGN: David Miller

CHIEF PHOTO EDITOR: Angela Gottschalk

CHIEF COPY EDITOR: John B. Saul

PROJECT MANAGER: Evelyn Edens

ASSISTANT EDITORS: Bill Reader, Rick Lund, Don Shelton

REPORTING: Steve Kelley, José Miguel Romero, Greg Bishop, Chris Cluff, Stuart Eskenazi, Bud Withers, Bob Condotta, Larry Stone, Jayda Evans, Craig Smith, John Boyle, Blaine Newnham

PHOTOGRAPHY: Rod Mar (lead), Dean Rutz, John Lok, Mike Siegel, Jim Bates, Steve Ringman, Dustin Snipes

SPORTS DESK: Mark McTyre, Tony Augusty, Jerry Faull, Scott Hanson, Dwight Perry, Carlyn Foster, Tony Guadagnoli, Jeff King, Joshua Beach, Mart Koivastik, Steve Dominguez, Jeff Paslay, Mark Akins

PHOTO PRODUCTION SPECIALISTS: Jessica Oyanagi, Heather Trimm, Ed Sauer

PHOTO EDITING: Barbara Kinney, Fred Nelson, Barry Fitzsimmons

TECH SUPPORT: Greg Anderson

STATISTICS: Mark Yuasa, Chester Chastek, Donald Dirks

COLOR IMAGING: Craig Brasch

SPECIAL ACKNOWLEGEMENTS: Cyndi Nash, Heidi de Laubenfels, Janet Farnam

The Seattle Times

seattletimes.com